The

Inscrutable

Mrs. Winchester

and

Her *Mysterious* Mansion

Lisa L. Selby

PublishAmerica
Baltimore

First printing

At the specific preference of the author, PublishAmerica allowed this work to remain exactly as the author intended, verbatim, without editorial input.

All photos courtesy of the Winchester Mystery House

ISBN: 1-4241-1374-1
PUBLISHED BY PUBLISHAMERICA, LLLP
www.publishamerica.com
Baltimore

Printed in the United States of America

This book is dedicated to the memory of two special people who I miss and love very much. First to my father, Ralph L. Selby and secondly, to my grandmother, Amy F. Burhans, who gave me love and encouragement in all my endeavors. I will be forever grateful. Lastly, this book is dedicated to the memory of Sarah L. Winchester, without whom, this book would never have been written, and who has mystified us all for over 100 years.

Acknowledgement

I wish to acknowledge Mr. Shozo Kagoshima, General Manager of the Winchester Mystery House, who answered my first letter with a polite, informative and encouraging reply. Special thanks goes to Cheryl Hamilton, Marketing Coordinator of the Winchester Mystery House. I relied on her for accurate information whenever I had discrepancies from other sources. Thanks for setting me straight and answering all my e-mail inquiries. It was an invaluable source of information I could not have done without. My thanks go to the late Ralph Rambo who wrote his eyewitness account of Sarah Winchester, "Lady of Mystery."

Introduction

Being born and raised in San Jose, California, the hometown of the Winchester Mystery House, I have had the opportunity to visit it several times. Each time I am fascinated, awestruck, and amazed at both the beauty and eccentricities of the house. I have felt a strong pull towards that house since my first visit at the age of seven. Its story and the woman behind the architectural wonder cast its spell on me. Ironically, my grandmother, who lived only a few blocks from what is now South Winchester Boulevard, never visited the house.

Perhaps no one will ever have all the answers, much less the real ones, behind the building of the house. It is not my intent to claim that what is written is the gospel truth. However, with discrepancies in regards to research information I have tried to weed fact from fiction, reality from myth in order to find the essential clues and meanings of this beautiful, and bizarre house. Concerning facts, I have relied more on eyewitness accounts for accuracy than second-hand information. Especially helpful was the book *Lady of Mystery (Sarah Winchester)* by Ralph Rambo, son of one of Mrs. Winchester's gardeners. I have also had to make judgment calls when various sources contained conflicting information on the same fact or topic, while trying to be as accurate as possible. In the last chapter, I analyze my theories and ideas regarding the truth. They are my opinions and do not reflect the beliefs held by the Winchester Mystery House or anyone else associated with it. Read it for yourself and draw your own conclusions. Perhaps the Winchester Mystery House will remain just that, a mystery. Enjoy!

Contents

Preface

When the Winchester repeating rifle was invented, who could believe it would lead to a sprawling mansion full of mystery, superstition, and oddities on the West Coast? Probably no one could have fathomed it, not even the Boston spiritualist Mrs. Winchester consulted one day.

Mrs. Sarah Winchester, née Sarah Lockwood Pardee, was born in New Haven, Connecticut circa 1838 or 1839. She was one of three daughters of Leonard and Sarah Burns Pardee, her father's occupation being that of a carriage manufacturer. She was a handsome woman with wavy brown hair arranged in the style of the day and large brown eyes. She was a diminutive 4' 10" and weighed approximately 100 pounds. Sarah, who spoke four languages fluently, was an accomplished musician, an avid reader, as well as an enthusiastic gardener.

On September 30, 1862, during the turmoil of the Civil War, she married William Wirt Winchester, heir to the Winchester Repeating Arms Company. Her husband was the only son of Oliver Fisher Winchester and the Vice-President of the company. Four years after their marriage, Sarah gave birth to a child on June 15, 1866, named Annie Pardee Winchester. Scarcely a month later, on July 24th, she died of a rare disease called marasmus. It is a form of malnutrition caused by either an insufficient food supply or the failure to absorb it, this in turn, causes the gradual wasting of tissues, and eventually death. Her husband took over the Presidency upon his father's death in 1880. His own death was soon to follow on March 7, 1881 due to Pulmonary Tuberculosis. Anyone would be devastated by the loss of a child so young, and a husband who died at the age of forty-three; it would be only normal. However, what followed could hardly be called "normal."

Sarah's doctors and friends in Connecticut encouraged her to seek a milder climate. They suggested she find a hobby to which she could devote her time. Something that would help her deal with her intense grief, in hopes of diminishing it. During this time, she sought Boston spiritualist, Adam Coons. As legend has it, the spiritualist told Mrs. Winchester that she was cursed by those killed via the Winchester repeating rifle. He said they were seeking their revenge. Indeed, it was the reason for the death of both her beloved child and handsome husband, the psychic divulged. The only way of appeasing these angry spirits was to move to the West Coast, buy a house, and build on it continuously. If she did this, no harm would come to her via the vengeful spirits.

This is the bizarre, but true story of what culminated, due to an immense inheritance, the loss of loved ones and the advice of a spiritualist. Fact, myth, and legend are inextricably interwoven into a pattern that is a bizarre tapestry. Perhaps you can find the one thread and unravel the mystery.

The History of the Winchester Repeating Arms Company

Born in 1810, Oliver Fisher Winchester was not born into a wealthy family, as one might expect. In fact, it was just the opposite. His father, a Boston farmer, died, when both he and his twin brother Samuel were just a year old, leaving the family destitute.

At the age of seven, he helped his mother feed her family of five by working in the fields. He attended school in the wintertime, when it was too cold to work outdoors. He also spent time clerking in retail stores. In his teenage years, he learned the carpentry trade in which he was employed from 1830-1837 in Baltimore, Maryland. There he supervised construction of numerous buildings, homes, as well as a church. Later he moved to New Haven, Connecticut, opening a men's clothing store with his partner John Davies in 1840, which catered to upscale clientele. Later that year he manufactured men's shirts using an improved pattern. In 1848, he patented this design, opening a factory in New Haven, Connecticut. It was called the New Haven Shirt Manufactory Company. The Newhallville factory he owned covered more than five acres. Eventually he amassed a fortune from his successful business. In 1855, his company grossed $600,000.

Oliver F. Winchester, who realized the firearm industry was making great progress, wanted to invest some of his money. He finally decided to allocate part of his wealth in the Volcanic Arms Company, though he knew virtually nothing about the manufacturing of guns.

In 1857, the President of the Volcanic Arms Company died, sending it into receivership. It allowed Oliver Winchester, who owned a majority of stock, to take over the declining business. He served as both the President and Treasurer. Due to problems with the Volcanic repeating rifle, he changed the company's name. He hoped the new name, the New Haven Arms Company, would give the business a more positive identity.

In December 1866, the company changed its name to the Winchester Repeating Arms Company. The rifle that made the Winchester Repeating Arms Co. a household name has a lengthy and circuitous history. The rifle began as a design by Walter Hunt, who was a New York inventor. He patented a loaded bullet in 1848,which he called a "rocket ball." The lead ball had a plug in the base, covering the black powder and fulminating mercury. In 1849, he patented a repeating firearm, called the "Volitional Repeater." The gun's lever action brought the bullet from the tube up into the chamber, making it ready for firing. There were several shortcomings with this rifle. One drawback was that it was made from small, delicate parts, making it both hard to build and repair, as well as to operate. Another difficulty was, that only one finger could be used for the lever, owing to its small size. Due to the lack of funds needed to promote the gun, it was never mass-produced.

Later, gunsmith Lewis Jennings improved Hunt's design. He made it more reliable by simplifying the repeating mechanism, patented on December 25, 1849. It was called the Jennings Rifle. The long wooden barrel retained the small lever utilized in the previous model. Due to several factors, it was a commercial failure. One was its awkwardness, another problem was the rifle's ammunition was not powerful enough to kill big game or accurate enough for long range firing. Only 1,000 were made before the Robbins and Lawrence Company in Vermont halted production. However, the basic design and layout of this rifle was the prototype to the Great Grandfather of the Winchester rifle, the "Gun that Won the West."

The Jennings rifle caught the attention of two gunsmiths employed at the Robbins and Lawrence factory. Their names were Daniel Wesson and Horace Smith. Wesson, who was working at the factory in 1850, began experimenting with the Jennings rifle. Smith was hired at the same time and was brought in to help with its development. He was an established arms maker with his own shop in Norwich, Connecticut. From their research and experimentation came a new patent for a repeating firearm granted on February 14, 1854.

The two men formed a partnership, which is now the famous company of Smith and Wesson. They specialized in manufacturing handguns using the new lever action mechanism from Smith's shop. The lever was now held by two fingers, instead of one, and the rifle held by a full hand, with the lever swinging forward. This is a typical characteristic of all Winchester lever-actions. It loaded as many as 30 bullets into the tube beneath the barrel, commonly referred to as the magazine. The rapid-fire capabilities of this gun gave it the trade name, "The Volcanic." A shoulder stock could be attached to the long handled pistol so that it resembled a rifle. Some advantages to the gun was that it was light, compact, could be loaded in less than a minute and had waterproof ammunition.

In 1855, Smith and Wesson were looking for people to invest in their company. They made an iron-framed lever action repeating rifle for demonstration purposes, hoping it would promote their business and attract venture capital. The 1854 patent, and the manner in which the gun was manufactured, contained the primary design typical of the gun for years to come.

Smith and Wesson, in order to promote their business further, renamed the company after their new invention. They called it the "The Volcanic Arms Company." At this time, forty local businessmen, including clockmakers, shoemakers, bakers and grocers, invested in the newly renamed company. One of these investors was Oliver F. Winchester, buying 800 shares for $25 each. He knew absolutely nothing about firearms, yet he was perceptive enough to see that the industry was making great progress and decided to invest in the boom.

The cartridge of the Volcanic consisted of a hollow based lead bullet, with a very small powder charge, making it incapable of traveling great distances or have any kind of hitting effect. It was good in theory, but turned out to be commercially unsuccessful. The Volcanic sales were poor and with the company falling into debt, most investors pulled out, including Smith and Wesson. They were more interested in developing revolvers than rifles.

It was at this time Oliver Winchester was left in control of the company in 1856. Feeling that the problems of the Volcanic might be averted by a name change, he turned the Volcanic Arms Company into the New Haven Arms Company in 1857. He employed 50 machinists and gunsmiths, as well as a team of women who worked in the ammunitions department. He used testimonials in his advertisements in order to persuade dealers to carry his firearms. Despite advertising, sales remained low due to its weak ammunition.

At that time, guns were in great demand due to the rumors of the pending Civil War and the expansion occurring in the West. This made him hasten to develop the perfect gun and cartridge. It needed to be powerful, dependable, and profitable. Winchester realized that the future of the rifle was to make and sell as many as possible for federal use.

Winchester found a designer to solve the gun's problem. In 1859, he hired Benjamin Tyler Henry as Superintendent of the Plant. Henry had been an apprentice gunsmith since he was sixteen years old, working in various New England gun shops, as well as the Springfield Armory. He had been the master mechanic at the Winchester Shirt Manufactory Company in the 1850s. His job there was to repair and maintain the foot pedal sewing machines on the production floor, all 500 of them.

Benjamin Henry experimented with new cartridge designs and a new repeating rifle, based upon the Volcanic mechanism design. He invented a rifle that fired larger, more powerful ammunition, naming it the Henry repeating rifle. It was both easy to use and very reliable, making it the first practical lever-action rifle ever made. When the throw lever came back, the hammer was already cocked with a new cartridge inserted into the breech. The magazine, under the barrel, fed by a spring, allowed the fresh cartridge to be loaded.

He patented it in 1860, giving the ownership to Winchester's New Haven Arms Company. Manufacture of the rifle began in 1861. A new metallic .44 caliber cartridge was made during this period. The powder, contained in a copper shell, had the bullet placed on top of it. Once fired, the bullet moved forward through the barrel, while the shell casing would remain in the barrel's breech where it could be extracted. The newly designed the cartridge was easier to carry and could be stored loosely in a box. These cartridges were also waterproof and loading was fast and efficient. The first Henry rifles came on the market in 1862, with the capability of discharging 14 to 15 times a minute. Due to its unproven reliability and non-standard ammunition, it was slow to be accepted by the Federal Ordinance of Officers.

People who were living on or crossing the dangerous frontier needed a means of survival, as well as a means of self-defense against wild animals, unfriendly Native Americans, bandits and the like. The Henry rifle soon became a familiar part of the Western frontier, and by 1866 the New Haven Arms Co. had made 13,000 of them. At one time, the rifle was so popular that the company was called the Henry Repeating Rifle Co. for one year.

On July 1, 1865 a new factory opened in Bridgeport, Connecticut, with its main goal to improve the Henry rifle. The rifle's major shortcoming was the slit cut along the lower edge of the magazine that allowed it to be loaded. This design allowed dirt to get into the weapon. The continual build-up of dirt eventually caused the rifle to fail. There were other problems as well, one was the rifle barrel got hot enough to burn the rifleman's hands. Secondly, it proved futile for long-range shooting since the ammunition lacked power to kill big game.

In 1866, the New Haven Arms Co. changed its name to the

Winchester Repeating Arms Company. Several changes were made to the Henry rifle, one being the conversion of the metal forearm to wood, allowing the person to handle the rifle when it got hot. The new patent on the loading gate allowed it to be loaded much quicker, and it did not have to be moved in order to do so. The company had strong sales for this model and 170,000 were made.

The Native Americans nicknamed this gun "Yellow Boy," due to all the brass used on the frame, the receiver, and other portions of the gun. This rifle model was used by the Sioux Indians at Little Big Horn against General George Armstrong Custer. They annihilated the Seventh U. S. Cavalry because their weapons were Winchester repeating rifles, while the ones used by the Cavalry were single shot rifles.

In 1873, the cartridge had been beefed up, giving it a lot more power. It was the first center-fire or "central fire" round as it was called then, thus named, because the primer was located in the center of the round than around the rim. These cartridges held one-third more black powder than before, enabling it to bring down large game such as buffalo. The gun frame had also been changed from brass to iron, the stronger materials making it more reliable under hard use. Its removable side panels allowed gunsmiths to work on the toggle bolt mechanism without having to completely disassemble the gun. The 1873 Model was the most popular rifle the company produced. During the years of 1873 to 1899, the height of frontier activity, there were over 540,000 Model 1873s manufactured. This model was popular with various groups of people, including lawmen, bandits, ranchers, and sportsmen. Even children were taught to shoot using the Winchester Model 1873.

Many famous and notorious people used "The Gun that Won the West." Some of the infamous names in Western history include Billy the Kid, Frank and Jesse James, and female bandit Pearl Hart, who used it to rob stagecoaches in Arizona. On the other side of the law, William F. "Buffalo Bill" Cody used it to kill the numerous buffalo he boasted about, as well as employing it in his Wild West Show. Theodore Roosevelt used it in his hunting safaris. By 1880, over 100,000 lever-action rifles were sold. Long after the "West was Won," the firearm was still being mass-produced. This type of production was decades before Henry Ford had built his first automobile.

In 1866, Oliver Winchester entered local politics and was elected Lieutenant Governor of Connecticut. He was known as Governor Winchester to his friends and associates. During this time, he lived in grand style. He resided in a Victorian house on Prospect Street in New Haven, Connecticut with his wife Jane Ellen and his children Ann, Hannah, and William. The house is no longer there, but has been replaced by Yale Divinity School, though the wrought iron fence still surrounds the property. He had also been Presidential Elector at Large for Abraham Lincoln. In fact, Oliver Winchester gave President Lincoln the sixth Henry rifle to come out of his factory. It was gold plated and intricately engraved. Both Secretary of War Edwin M. Stanton and the Secretary of the Navy, Gideon Wells, were also given rifles from the Winchester factory.

In 1880, at the age of 70, Oliver Winchester died of a stroke, leaving behind a personal fortune worth one and a half million dollars. His son William, who was Vice-President at the time, took over the Presidency upon his father's death. His time was short-lived however, when he succumbed to pulmonary tuberculosis on March 7, 1881 at the age of 43. Taking over for William Winchester was William Converse, who remained President of the Company until 1890.

In 1886, John Browning, one of the most productive and brilliant inventors in gun making history, joined the Winchester Repeating Arms Co. He started with a single shot rifle developed in 1886. The Winchester Repeating Arms Co. used his patents to help make the lever action stronger. Because of this improvement, it was able to withstand the pressure of larger, more powerful black powder cartridges, without being too long, too heavy, or too complicated. He used a mechanism on which the loading lever pivoted directly on a longitudinally sliding breech and bolt. This design, meeting all of Winchester's specifications, gave the '86 operating action a stronger breech than was necessary. The new lever action could take the most powerful cartridge known at that time, discharging it with both speed and accuracy.

A high performance black powder ammunition was introduced in 1899. It had a relatively light bullet with a very light charge. The trajectory of 300 yards was extremely flat, making long-range shooting of 800 to 900 yards perfectly feasible. It had a capacity of eight or nine cartridges and was used for shooting big game in the United States and Africa. The gun was capable of felling grizzly bears, moose, rhinos, and even elephants. It was offered for sale at $45 and within a short span of time, became one of Winchester's most successful rifles. One problem with this model was the cost of manufacturing it, making it comparatively expensive to purchase. It was for this reason; Winchester simplified its design and reintroduced it as the Model 1894.

It looked very similar to the previous models. The difference being, that it had a nickel steel barrel and included a very heavy sliding breechblock mortised into the receiver. This enabled it to have the strength needed to handle the chamber pressures generated by the new smokeless powders. The advantage of the relatively small-caliber bullets was the capability to reach velocities in excess of 2,000 feet per second. The Model 1894 was so successful that it is still widely used today.

Two companies, Spencer and Winchester, had been the first to begin a trend towards repeating firearms. However, these two companies were not the only successful gun manufacturers. Influenced by the success of the Winchester 1873, the Colt Company decided to compete with them for gun sales. In 1883, the Colt Co. manufactured a lever-action rifle, similar in design to that of the Winchester.

The Colt-Burgess had a simplified mechanism designed by Andrew Burgess. A breech-lever extension was combined with a longitudinally sliding breechblock. When the breech was locked, the breech-lever pivot pin took the pressure that the explosive cartridge generated. This gun was able to chamber the popular .45-.75 cartridge used by the Government. Its tubular shaped magazine held between eight to ten rounds and was available in a variety of barrel lengths, weights, set triggers, engravings and target sights. It was also manufactured in a lightweight version, selling at $24 for a carbine, $27 for a rifle and $1 more for every extra inch for long barreled rifles. This gun proved to be a success, which annoyed the Winchester Company. In an attempt to convince the Colt Co. to halt production of this rifle, they threatened to manufacture pistols in direct competition with the Colt Company's singular action.

Winchester had purchased some of Burgess's promising designs, and by holding the rights to an improved Burgess rifle; they could very easily follow through on their threat. The two companies finally came to agreement; Winchester would not pursue the manufacturing of pistols, while Colt agreed to discontinue the manufacturing of rifles. There were 6,400 Colt-Burgess rifles manufactured within the span of a year. Colt later manufactured rifles, however, they concentrated on a different aspect of the repeating rifle market so as not to compete directly with the Winchester Company. Despite the competition from other gun manufacturers, Winchester had a dominant hold on the lever-action rifle market. They sold more rifles than all the arms manufacturers combined.

The Model 1895 was designed with the new smokeless powder specifically in mind, which had made its appearance the previous year. A posse bringing three of these rifles with them, captured Butch Cassidy and the Sundance Kid.

During this time, Thomas Gary Bennett was the fourth President, from 1890-1910. The U.S. Government purchased Winchester rifles to be used in the Spanish-American War of 1898. They also purchased rifles for WWI when George E. Hodson was President from 1911-1915. The sixth President of the Winchester Repeating Arms Company was Winchester Bennett who was in charge from 1915-1919.

After WWI, the company implemented a Post-war program focusing on the manufacturing of new products. The idea behind this was to fill the factory space previously used for military production. At one point in time, there were 6,300 individually owned Winchester stores carrying their products, making them the largest hardware chain store organization in

LISA L. SELBY

the world. They manufactured merchandise for outdoor use such as Winchester flashlights, boys' wagons, bicycles, footballs, fishing tackle, and roller skates. They also produced household goods such as iceboxes, scissors, cutlery, food choppers, pots and pans, meat grinders, and electric irons. Tools such as planers, hammers, and axes, as well as lawn mowers, farm and garden tools were also made by the company.

Franklin W. Olin, founder of Equitable Cartridge Co., later changed its name to the Western Cartridge Co. in 1898. The Winchester Repeating Arms Co., having gone into receivership in 1931, due to their expansion in the hardware industry, was sold to the Western Cartridge Company. Soon afterwards, the Western Cartridge Co. scaled down the newly purchased company to its main industry of arms and ammunition. During WWII Winchester-Western made 15 billion rounds of ammunition and developed the U.S. carbine and M-1 rifle. At the end of the war, there were 62,000 employees, some working in government factories. Winchester, now one of three divisions of the Olin Co., sold its rifle making operations in New Haven in 1981 to the U.S. Repeating Arms Corporation and was licensed to make Winchester rifles and shotguns. The Winchester division of Olin Industries still manufactures its ammunition. Olin Industries also make copper alloys and other metals, chlorine and caustic soda. They have also become involved in aerospace technology.

The Life of Sarah Winchester, Fact and Fiction

After the death of her daughter in 1866 and the death of her husband in 1881, it would not be surprising if Sarah Winchester thought she was cursed. In those days, the occult was a popular entertainment, with séances, tarot cards, palm readings, spiritualists, and planchette boards. Therefore, when a friend suggested Mrs. Winchester consult a medium, it is not surprising that she took the advice seriously.

In a trance, the spiritualist informed Sarah that her deceased husband was in the room, and even described him. Supposedly, her husband told her there was a curse on the Winchester family that was responsible for taking not only their baby daughter's life, but his as well. This misfortune was derived from the people killed by the Winchester Rifle. According to the medium, Adam Coons, they were seeking revenge, and unless she sold her property in New Haven, Connecticut and moved West, the curse would take her too. She was told her husband would guide her to her new home, which she would recognize when she saw it. Sarah was informed that she had to build on the house continuously or be haunted by those killed by the Winchester rifle.

William Wirt Winchester

As a result, in 1884 she traveled across country, arriving at a spot three miles West of what was then, the small town of San Jose, California. There she discovered an eight-room farmhouse, owned by Dr. Caldwell, already under construction. She negotiated the purchase of the house, and the land surrounding it for $12,500 in gold coin. It was situated in a rural area on what was then Los Gatos Road. (It was to become South Winchester Boulevard after her death.)

She had no problem whatsoever in being able to afford the house. Her husband, upon his death, left her several million dollars in cash, (some reports quote the figure at $20 million) and 777 shares of stock in the Winchester Repeating Arms Company. When her mother-in-law died in 1897, she received from her will 2,000 more shares of stock, thus giving her 48.8 percent of the company's stock. Before the days of income tax, she received $1,000 a day from her shares of stock. Regardless of figures in dollars and cents or shares of stock, what was important, was that she had enough money to build continuously on her house without fear of depleting her entire inheritance.

Her arrival in the area caused a sensation with the locals. No doubt there had never been a millionairess in their midst, so, it was not surprising that the town took a personal interest in this "celebrity." They were both curious and fascinated by their new resident. Understandably, they were intrigued by the freight cars, belonging to Mrs. Winchester; curious as to what objects they held. These cars were shuttled to sidetracks at the train station in Santa Clara until they could be unloaded and the items brought to her residence.

Undoubtedly, the townspeople were astonished, as they watched the amazing rate of building activity during the first six months of her residency. The townspeople saw an eight-room farmhouse burst into a twenty-six-room mansion during that span of time. It was motivation enough to set the townspeople to talking and speculating about reasons behind the furious pace. Local gossip turned into rumors, which, over the years, have added to the legend of this mysterious lady. Some of these stories are false, while some hold a grain of truth. They are so interwoven after numerous years of retelling, that it is sometimes difficult to sift truth from fiction. True or not, they have stuck as fact to the lady known as Sarah Winchester. Reality has become blurred and the facts distorted or lost in the legend of the Winchester Mystery House. Here are some of the tall tales that have grown out of control, much like the house itself.

One such story spread by the townspeople, dealt with her reason for settling in California. Supposedly, it was due to the loss of her husband and child during a fire in a Connecticut thunderstorm. Visiting a spiritualist after this devastating tragedy, she was advised to take a trip around the world. While on her journey she visited mediums, spiritualists, and yogis in both Europe and India. This was when, according to some people, she had been informed of the curse on the Winchester family. She was told that in order to appease avenging spirits, she was to build continuously on a house in the West or she would die. Upon her return from her world tour, she arrived in San Francisco, allegedly settling in Santa Clara Valley because it had fewer thunderstorms than in her home state.

In the case of her infant daughter, she had not died in a fire, but rather from a rare disease, called marasmus, a form of malnutrition. Her husband died fifteen years later, not in a fire, but due to pulmonary tuberculosis.

Another story around town took place during the early part of her residency. She sent out gold lettered invitations to all the prominent people in the area for a reception to be held at her home. It was to be a magnificent dinner with a variety of delicacies from almost every part of the country. She even attempted to hire the well-known orchestra, "The Bostonians" for the occasion. However, they already had an engagement in San Francisco and refused her offer of $3,000! It was said that she waited until midnight, but no one came. This was supposedly both the reason and the time she became a recluse, but the story was a complete fabrication as the townspeople could attest.

It was true however, that several neighborhood women planned to make a social call on their newest resident. They were met with a firm no, never having stepped a foot inside the door.

There was also a rumor that President Theodore Roosevelt, an ardent fan and owner of a Winchester rifle, was to pass by the house. His destination was the nearby town of Campbell, where he was to plant the now famous Redwood tree in 1903. One story claimed that he sent her a message saying he would stop by to pay his respects. Some people said the President knocked on the double doors at the front entrance, but no one answered. One of the gardeners who did not recognize him, told him to go to the back door "just like everyone else." The President, insulted, stalked away angrily.

The Inscrutable Mrs. Winchester
and Her Mysterious Mansion

Yet another version said the San Jose Chamber of Commerce tried to arrange a visit for President Roosevelt. Mrs. Winchester, however, turned them down with a sharp "no!" The only thing that is certain is that President Roosevelt did pass by her house. Ralph Rambo, who was a kid at the turn of the century, was an eyewitness and wrote about the account in his book, *Lady of Mystery (Sarah Winchester)*.

However, not everyone was refused admittance to this architectural wonder. She did allow young people to visit. Senior citizens, years after Sarah Winchester's death, related stories of the parties Mrs. Winchester would hold in her garden. They told of a flower-laden landscape bordered by rare dwarf boxwood while ornamental trees and bushes shaded the lush gardens. They spoke of "Strawberry Hill" where Mrs. Winchester's maids served them French ice cream, made with real cream. She had a great affection for little girls, letting them play in her house, as well as on her rosewood grand piano that was located in the Grand Ballroom. No doubt, they were emotional replacements for her deceased daughter whom she missed. Their companionship on these visits probably gave her joy and comfort, easing some of her pain and loneliness.

Her favorite niece, Miss Marian Isabel Merriman, born only a couple of years after Sarah's daughter, was also a constant companion, as well as her secretary. She stayed with her aunt in what is called the Oriental room, probably until she married. Sarah's sister Isabel Merriman was allowed entrance to her home as well.

Few other people were allowed entrance into her mysterious mansion. One of these people was Mary Baker Eddy, founder of the Church of Christ, Scientist in 1879. The Christian Scientists believed in physical healing, not through medicinal means, but through spiritual means. Mary Baker Eddy had taken a serious fall on the ice in 1866. She chose to cure herself by reading a biblical revelation and was healed. What significance her visit had is unknown. Perhaps it was to help Mrs. Winchester with her arthritis or some other ailment she might have had.

Some said Sarah Winchester was a Spiritualist, while a few insisted she was a Theosophist, though she never admitted it.

She had been raised as an Episcopalian and had a Baptist minister officiate her husband's funeral. Henrietta Sivera, a constant companion, denied Mrs. Winchester had any spiritualist leanings. This leaves one to wonder if the stories about séances, ghosts, and other superstitions are valid.

Rumors that Mrs. Winchester was a recluse spread around town, but this is not true. It was typical of well-to-do widows in those days to spend the remainder of their lives in mourning. Consequently, she was not supposed to entertain inside or outside her home. Her name was well known about town and she was well liked. Yet, this did not keep rumors from spreading like wild fire around the area, some from the townspeople, some from strangers. Her niece told her about the stories being spread. Mrs. Winchester however, was very sensitive to this kind of talk and didn't like the dramatic things said about her. She was not only upset, but also hurt by these thoughtless, fabricated stories. Still, many believed she was a recluse, hiding behind the solid cypress hedge surrounding her property.

This hedge was allegedly backed up with barbed wire fencing, according to local gossip. It was said there was a pack of ferocious dogs patrolling the grounds as well, with a staff of armed guards to protect her. Mr. Rambo, one of the groundskeepers, helped with much of the landscaping, planting many of the ornamental trees and pruning the cypress hedge. He never mentioned any barbed wire fence. Neither did the man who later removed the hedge decades later. Therefore, it is equally unbelievable that she had either armed guards or dogs patrolling the grounds. The rumor is probably due to someone's over-active imagination, which grew in the telling.

Along the lines of privacy, it was reported that Mrs. Winchester wore a dark veil everywhere she went, even inside her home. The only person who ever saw her face was the Chinese butler as he served her meals. There is a story that two workers passed her in one of the many hallways, accidentally catching a glimpse of her face. For the infraction they were fired and given years pay. This is just another one of the many fictional stories that have persisted over the years regarding

Sarah Winchester. Certainly, there was no reason for her to wear a veil inside the house, where the only ones who saw her were her servants, her niece, her sister, and the few guests who entered her house. It would also be stifling to wear a veil with the numerous heat sources she had in her house.

It was believed that she was averse to having her picture taken. One story regarding this topic, concerned several newspapermen attempting to set up their cameras on the grounds of her estate. She was gathering flowers in her garden without a veil, when she suddenly noticed them. Rushing into the dehydrator to avoid them, she almost suffocated. According to legend, more guards and watchdogs were brought in for protection around the clock. This incident never happened; it is merely another story to add to the legend of Sarah Winchester.

There are, in fact, a few photos of Mrs. Winchester in existence, contrary to popular belief. One is a black and white photo, taken in her early years, in which she wears a white blouse with a ruffled collar. Yet, another painted photo was taken at Tabler Photo Studio on 124 Post Street in San Francisco, California. The most well known photo, taken in her later years, shows her seated in her carriage in front of her house. She is wearing a small, flat hat atop her gray hair; there is no veil whatsoever on the hat and her face is clearly visible. If she supposedly wore a veil everywhere, then this picture dispels the myth. She wears a cape with its collar up around her neck; on her lap is a blanket covering her lower torso. She appears to be looking in the direction of the photographer. According to legend, the photo was allegedly taken without her knowledge by one of her gardeners hiding behind a hedge. This tale of the hidden gardener, is yet another one of the famous stories that has followed the Winchester legend over the years. In those days, cameras were large boxes set on tripods, with a black curtain covering the photographer as he took the picture. Flash powder was also used, making not only a noise, but smoke as well. Therefore, it would have been impossible for her not to notice her photo being taken. In addition, taking photos at that time was not the quick process it is today. The subject had to hold very still so the photo could be taken, otherwise it would be blurred. Therefore, Mrs. Winchester had to know that she was having her picture taken, that and the slight smile that seems to be on her grandmotherly looking face, gives evidence of that.

Mrs. Winchester in her carriage.

Presumably, Mrs. Winchester slept in a different room every night to elude vengeful spirits trying to harm her. This is yet another rumor turned to legend. She slept in only two bedrooms. One was her favorite bedroom, the Daisy bedroom, at the front of the house. She slept in this room until the advent of the 1906 Earthquake. After the quake, she slept in a room that overlooked the back gardens and a crescent-shaped hedge.

Supposedly, there were only two mirrors in the house. This was due to the fact, that ghosts do not like mirrors since they are unable to cast a reflection. However, in actuality, there are several mirrors in the house. There is one in the Grand Ballroom, one in the morning room, one in her niece's bedroom, one in her bedroom, one in the parlor and several in storage.

Yet, another tall tale arose regarding her meals. Mrs. Winchester, it was said, dined either alone or with her niece, Miss Marion Merriman. Supposedly she dined every evening on a $30,000 gold plated set of dishes. These plates were said to be kept in a safe, with Sarah counting them as they were removed, and doing the same upon their return, making certain all the plates were accounted for.

There is one anecdote, that while dining in luxurious fashion with her niece, Sarah wanted to serve one of her vintage wines stored in the wine cellar. Possessing the only key, she went down the cellar stairs; upon her arrival, she was terrified to find a black handprint on one of the walls. Horrified, she immediately ran up the cellar stairs and into the house without the bottle. That night, the spirits told her the handprint belonged to that of a demon. Mrs. Winchester, taking this as a warning sign against alcoholic spirits, ordered the cellar walled up. It was walled up so well, according to legend, that the wine cellar has never been found. This is yet another story, no doubt promulgated by the townspeople's gossip. No wine cellar has ever been found. If she had stored wine in a cellar, it has long since disappeared from its storage place. There are only two basements on her estate, one with a coal furnace and a boiler to make steam for the radiators. She stored food in these basements, possibly wine, but no black handprint was ever found after her death.

Sarah had 52 skylights in her house, purportedly used to spy on her servants. For instance, one skylight looks down into the kitchen, as popular opinion has it, to see if her servants were trying to poison her. It was also said she would creep up behind them to watch them work. One such account, said she was making certain her servants were working and not gossiping about her. While it is believed she spied on her servants, in all likelihood, it was to make sure they were performing their duties properly. Paying them twice the normal rate, she no doubt insisted on their loyalty, and expected them to work hard. However, it is a far-fetched belief that she thought any of her servants would poison her. If she had any fear of this, she certainly would have fired them and not been as generous to them as she was. Her philanthropy was evidenced by giving them money or real estate, as well as letting them live on her property rent-free.

Yet, another tale involved passersby hearing music emanating from her home after midnight. Some thought it came from the spirits haunting her house. In actuality, it was none other than Mrs. Winchester, playing to exercise stiff, arthritic fingers or merely because her arthritis was keeping her awake at night. However, with her estate of 161 acres and the house being set back from the street by a large yard, it is unlikely passersby would have heard the music.

There were also tales of midnight séances where she would make her way through a labyrinth of rooms and hallways. According to one account, upon pressing a button, a panel would fly back, allowing her to step from one apartment into another. Then she would open a window in that apartment, climbing out onto a flight of stairs, taking her down one story until she met another flight of stairs, bringing her right back to the level she had started on. After traveling through a maze of more stairs, supposedly touching her foot on every one, she came to a great room, filled with balconies. Some of these balconies allowed her to step through a window only to find herself on the same balcony. From there, she entered a door that once closed, could not be opened from the inside. After following a circuitous route for a half hour or so, a path designed to confuse any evil spirits who might be following her, she came to a clothes press in one of the mansion's bedrooms. The two bottom drawers and one of the clothes press doors are false. The other door leads not into a closet, but into the séance room. While there were three entrances into this room, there was only one exit. She had to leave through a narrow door, stepping over a bar a foot and a half high, from the floor. One of the three doors in the room opened onto a skylight to the room below, definitely not one of the ways to exit the room. It was said that only she had the key to the room and would wear it around her neck. Yet it served as a room where the chauffeur and later the head gardener and his wife, used it as their residence, thus posing a question about her séances. Neighbors reported they heard a bell toll at the hour of midnight to call the spirits to her séance. They also heard the bell ring at one and two o'clock a.m., supposedly to have the spirits return to their resting place.

In the séance room are thirteen hooks, nine behind the cupboard's two doors and four on the wall next to the cupboard. As rumor has it, she hung thirteen different colored robes decorated with occult symbols used for her séances. In this room, she supposedly had a table on which a planchette board, similar to today's Ouija board, was placed. Her hand resting on the indicator atop the planchette board, moved around, pointing to letters and spelling out messages from the spirits. The architectural ideas given by the spirits were then written down on paper, tablecloths, napkins, or brown paper bags. She never commissioned an architect to draw a blueprint for the house. The only plans used for its construction were her drawings. The original blue print she received, upon purchase of the house from Doctor Caldwell, was thrown out. She also consulted her collection of architectural books, technical books, magazines, and engineering plans. These reference books she kept handy in her library next door.

She gave the plans to her foreman John Hansen; while some sources say her secretary-niece Mrs. Marion Merriman

Marriott performed this task. Everyday Sarah would stroll the grounds with her foreman, during these walks, she would stop to use a sawhorse as a drawing table. There she would draw new plans on the backs of old envelopes or brown paper bags.

Some of the plans were chaotic, however, they showed a flair for building. Sometimes the plans that were designed wouldn't work out the way she had intended, but she never became discouraged. When she discovered the construction from the previous day didn't work, she ordered it torn down, changed, built around, or merely ignored the mistakes. This could be one of the explanations for the bizarre features of the house. The most famous, well-known reason, was the spirits guiding her plans through séances. Some of the home's unusual features are stairs that stop inches from the ceiling, there are also bars on inside windows of the house and corridors that lead to a dead end. Even the original back porch steps from the eight-room farmhouse still exist within the house. She simply built around them as construction continued.

Some people, in order to explain the house's oddities, said she was trying to confuse the spirits with bizarre architectural features. These features include pillars installed upside down on the front porch, fireplaces and newel posts on the stairways. In addition, a chimney rises four floors stopping eighteen inches below the ceiling, making the fireplaces below obsolete. This anomaly occurred because the fourth floor was not completely roofed in for a number of years, during this time the chimney was fully functional. When she finally extended the roof, she failed to do the same with the chimney.

Employees of Mrs. Winchester said that she was strong-minded, firm, yet always fair, and kind. They also told about her deep, genuine concern regarding their family's welfare. The typical rate of pay at the time was a dollar and a half a day. Sarah, on the other hand, paid her employees three dollars a day! They were not only well paid, but were rewarded with gifts of real estate, homes, and even lifetime pensions. They also lived on her estate rent-free. One of her workers' sons said she would not tolerate laziness, stealing, gossip, or revealed confidences. Mrs. Winchester, he said, expected them to perform their work to her strict standards and specifications. If she found any servants participating in these activities, they would be fired.

Yet, if they were faithful, loyal and hardworking, she was certain to reward them. As evidence of their loyalty, many of the workers usually stayed 15 to 20 years. One carpenter stayed for 36 years, while another spent 33 years doing nothing but building, installing, and tearing up floors.

The chimney to nowhere.

For example, when the 1909 Renault she owned (which she paid $8,400 for) had mechanical difficulties, she called in a mechanic from San Francisco; his name was Fred Larson. After fixing the car, she offered him a job with a high salary, but he declined. Mrs. Winchester continued to persist, asking him to name his price. Fred, quoting an outrageous amount, assumed she would refuse. He was very much surprised, however, when she accepted his request. He was yet another example of her loyal employees, working for Mrs. Winchester until her death.

Sarah occasionally tested the loyalty of her workers. One account concerned a painter she had employed. She told him to paint an entire room, ceiling included, in red enamel. Three days later, she asked him to paint the same room white.

Another test occurred while deciding whom to hire for the gardener's position. Mrs. Winchester asked three applicants to plant a row of cabbages upside down. The first person followed her instructions, the second person refused. The third person agreed, but suggested they be planted properly, right side up. The third applicant was hired. No doubt, Sarah had reasons for testing her workers. She might have wanted to see just how intelligent they were, what amount of common sense they had, how well they followed instructions, in addition to the loyalty they had towards her.

Mrs. Sarah Winchester

The Inscrutable Mrs. Winchester
and Her Mysterious Mansion

There was definitely a bond between her and her workers. It is evident in the way she signed the Christmas cards given to her employees, signing them Sarah L. Winchester, "Aunt Sadie." This signature demonstrated that she considered them not only her employees, but also her family as well. In fact, they were probably a substitute for the family she had lost. It is obvious she cared about them as more than mere servants and employees; evidenced by the gifts she gave them during her lifetime and in her will. After all, with the exception of her sister and her favorite niece, she had no relatives living nearby.

Leo Sullivan, an orchestra leader in the early days of the small town, worked at the Jose' and Victory Theaters. He told a story about Mrs. Winchester's French maid, who, on her night off, would attend a play or production, performed by a local stock company. Upon her return, she told Mrs. Winchester about that evening's performance. If Sarah was interested in a production, she would ask the players to perform excerpts from the play. These were performed often after midnight in her spacious ballroom. The performers happily granted her request, in view of her generosity.

Despite rumors to the contrary, Sarah Winchester was not mentally unbalanced, as some believed. In fact, she was an intelligent woman with an excellent memory. She knew the location of every item on her estate, keeping an inventory on everything down to the last screw. She once asked Fred Larson to fix a gate. He went to the storeroom, and finding some brass colored screws in a drawer used them for the needed repairs. Mrs. Winchester mentioned to Fred that six screws were missing from the storeroom and asked if he had taken them. He explained he'd used them to fix the gate. She informed him they were solid gold screws she had been saving for something special and asked him to use something cheaper in their place.

Sarah rode in the elegant conveyances of the era. Her first mode of transportation was a Victoria with liveried coachman. With the advent of the automobile, she purchased a French Renault in 1909, later a Buick "Town Car," and finally two Pierce Arrows, one painted in gold and lavender. Reportedly, she also purchased a yacht that was never used.

She would travel in one of her conveyances to go to the town's only shopping area along First Street. There she parked by the curb, remaining in her vehicle, probably because her arthritis was impeding her mobility. Merchants would bring their goods out for Mrs. Winchester's inspection. There she would purchase fine bolts of material, linens, and other necessities, always paying in gold, nothing was ever returned. One merchant, in order to accommodate Mrs. Winchester, built a drive through in his store, large enough for her carriage to enter.

She also spent money on real estate. It was said, a real estate agent leaked the news to one of her servants that an investor was planning to build a saloon across the street from her home. She purchased the land for an exorbitant amount, bringing her property to a total of 161 acres. Reportedly, she also purchased homes in Atherton, Palo Alto, Los Altos, and San Mateo. According to some sources, she never saw the houses she purchased, much less stepped inside them. The only homes she owned, besides Llanda Villa, at the time of her death, were the ones occupied by her sister Isabel, and her niece Marian. She may have told them she would purchase a house for both of them. This would explain why she never entered the houses before purchasing them.

From 1884 to 1906, the mansion rose from a one-story farmhouse to seven stories. The house itself consisted of four floors with an observation tower looming three stories above the mansion. On April 18, 1906, at 5:12 a.m., the San Francisco earthquake woke up Northern California. Mrs. Winchester was sleeping in her favorite "Daisy" bedroom, when portions of the observation tower came tumbling down, falling onto the room's chimney. Located on the same wall as the doorframe, the brick fireplace served as support for the wall. When the chimney dropped to the first floor, the wall shifted. This movement left Sarah's closed door jammed.

Her servants most likely raced out of the house in terror once the shaking stopped. They were no doubt worried about finding their family members in the aftermath, and had forgotten that Mrs. Winchester was still inside. Once things had calmed down, they made their way through the rubble and fallen objects, in order to reach her room at the front of the house. They probably spent at least an hour, if not more, getting to her. When they found Sarah, they had to pry open the jammed door using a crowbar. She was very much traumatized by this event. Not only did the quake damage the observation tower, but some of the cupolas and chimneys as well. It knocked off some of the plaster on the interior walls, including the Grand Ballroom, morning room, the Crystal room, and the Daisy room she was in at the time. After this catastrophic event, she built the house outwards and no higher than four stories. After her terrifying experience, she probably wanted no repetition of what occurred in 1906.

1906 earthquake damage.

According to legend, she thought the earthquake was a sign from the spirits, telling her she had spent too much money on the front portion of the house. She therefore ordered the front section of the house, a total of 30 rooms, boarded up in an attempt to appease them. These rooms included the Grand Ballroom, the Daisy bedroom, the Crystal room, the Front Parlor and two kitchens, as well as the newly installed double doors of the main entrance. She never used the front portion of the house again. One theory is that she was planning repairs at a later date, but never got around to it. On the other hand, she might not have wanted to be reminded of the harrowing event by using the damaged rooms again.

After the quake, she moved to a bayside barge in San Francisco for six months, allowing her workers to clean up the rubble and debris left in the Great Earthquake's aftermath. The workers had to make the necessary repairs before she could return permanently to her home. During that time, she sent a messenger to deliver her designs and building plans to the mansion.

The seven-story observation tower, probably used to overlook her orchard, garden, and the landscape, had been too damaged to repair. It was then torn down, never to be rebuilt. Perhaps, perceiving it unsafe, she decided not to build any higher than the four stories that remained after this natural disaster. After the earthquake, building continued, sprawling over the land as it wound leisurely around, reaching what was once a distant barn. With the continuous construction, the mansion finally surrounded the barn and became attached to it.

One might get the impression from the extensive construction of the house, the multitude of furnishings required, as well as the time and effort spent on her gardens and orchards, that she spent money only on herself. This was not true; she gave anonymously to various charities. There were eyewitnesses who watched her take daily trips delivering hot soup and food for a new resident on nearby Stevens Creek Road or for a man dying of tuberculosis. She also made annual trips to the Old Cupertino Church. There Mrs. Rambo, a member of the Ladies Aid Society (her husband a gardener at

Mrs. Winchester's residence), collected used clothing for the local poor children. Her son, Ralph Rambo, recalled seeing her liveried coachman disembarking from the polished Victoria. He was laboring with a huge hamper filled with clothes, as he climbed the church steps. They were not used clothes, as most people donated, but new ones.

Sarah wanted her charitable acts to remain unknown; thus, no one knows the full extent of her munificence. Nevertheless, even if her munificence to the community was never fully revealed, her benevolence to her servants was.

Yet, her greatest and most well known contribution was to the William Wirt Winchester Hospital. She had established the William Wirt Winchester Fund in 1909 purportedly giving $1,200,000 in his memory. Her money went to build a hospital dedicated to the care of tuberculosis patients. Land was purchased on Campbell Avenue in West Haven, Connecticut. Construction began in 1916, but, before it could be completed, the United States government leased the building, using it as a military hospital. In May of 1918, the William Wirt Winchester Hospital was dedicated, continuing to be leased by the government until 1927. It operated as the Tuberculosis Division of New Haven Hospital from 1928 to 1940. Eventually it was discontinued due to the decline in tuberculosis cases. The buildings were sold in 1948 to the government. In order to perpetuate the memorial, the name was transferred to the Hospital's former Private Pavilion. Today the William Wirt Winchester Fund helps patients with respiratory diseases at Yale-New Haven Hospital.

Although she rarely traveled, she did however; visit relatives in the Bay Area. This included her niece Mrs. Marion Merriman Marriott, who lived in Palo Alto, and her sister Isabel Merriman. Her one vacation was spent at the Del Monte Hotel in Monterey.

On the morning of September 5, 1922, she passed away in her sleep from heart failure. It was said that once the news of her death was announced, the workers stopped what they were doing, leaving nails partially driven into the wood. Her body was shipped back to New Haven in a $2,500 bronze casket for burial with her husband and daughter. She left behind her sister, Isabel Merriman, and numerous nieces and nephews, also grandnieces and grandnephews.

It is strange that with all the rumors spread about Mrs. Winchester, not a single relative ever gave an interview after her passing. No relative felt compelled to explain the house's oddities, the history behind it, or to defend Sarah Winchester and her sanity. Perhaps they respected her privacy. Maybe they had no patience for the impertinent, illogical questions that would be asked, due to the rumors that had spread throughout the town. They might have thought it best to ignore the gossip and crazy stories, hoping they would eventually die down and be forgotten.

There were others outside her immediate family, however, who did defend her. One person said it was "utterly false that she was an eccentric or mentally unbalanced." Another one claimed, "She was preyed on by people" and yet another, that " she was a sweet person and not at all crazy." "Her mind was perfectly clear at the end," someone said. In addition, her attorney R. F. Lieb said she was "as sane and clear-headed as any woman I have ever known. She has a better grasp of business and financial affairs than most men." He also didn't believe that she thought her continuous building would insure her everlasting life. These quotes came from acquaintances such as her foreman, John Hansen, Elmer Jensen, W.T. Creffield, as well as her attorney for many years, Roy F. Lieb and Dr. Clyde Wayland, her personal physician.

After her death, the safe was opened. Though it had been rumored that she had six safes set in cement, only one was found in the Grand Ballroom. In this safe, there was no gold plated dining service found or any other valuables. Instead, the only items found were some fishing line, socks, woolen underwear, newspaper clippings, and a lock of baby hair in a tiny, purple velvet box. There was also an article clipping from the New Haven newspaper inside. It was her daughter's obituary that read: "Winchester. In this city July 24, 1866. Annie Pardee, infant daughter of William Wirt and Sarah L. Winchester."

The Inscrutable Mrs. Winchester
and Her Mysterious Mansion

Mrs. Sarah Winchester never left a journal and she was never interviewed, thus leaving no concrete reason for the manner in which she built her house. Her attorney Roy F. Lieb said she built the vast estate in hopes her relatives would come to visit. This wish never materialized. All that is left are murky truths and some unsubstantiated myths interwoven into an inextricable design.

As for being considered a recluse, there are many reasons why she did not entertain the townspeople at her home. One reason could be that Mrs. Winchester wanted to be left alone with her inconsolable grief. According to social mores, being a widow, she was not allowed to entertain. She was also too busy running a household, overseeing gardens and orchards to spend time entertaining, even if she had had the inclination to do so.

One person said she was preyed on by people, as evidenced by her nephew's visit. A person with such a fortune as hers must have been susceptible to fortune hunters and con artists, not to mention well-meaning charities. This could partially explain the reason for her hiding behind a hedge, allowing only certain people into her home. She did allow children in, perhaps because children did not think about monetary matters, as did adults. They were no doubt more interested in playing on her piano, having ice cream parties, or playing in a large, beautiful garden such as hers. Having children around could also mitigate the loneliness she must have felt for her deceased child.

The stories or her life, fact or fiction, has been the cause of much interest and debate throughout the years. Whatever the reasons behind the building of her house, whether the advice of a spiritualist or her desire for a new start, her fascination with architecture, or a place for her relatives to visit, the mansion she left behind is something people continue to talk about, well over a century after her death. It is one of the most unique, architecturally beautiful houses ever built, if not the oddest.

The House

When Sarah Winchester purchased the house, she hired 10 to 22 carpenters to help her carry out her plans, 24 hours a day, 7 days a week, 365 days a year. There were no holidays as far as construction of the house was concerned. According to legend, she had to build continuously or she would die.

If indeed this story was true, then she followed the medium's orders out of fear. Possibly, she was afraid to be met by the spirits who had died via the Winchester rifle. Her apprehension may have resulted from guilty feelings of earning her wealth through their misfortune. Perhaps she was terrified of the revenge they might wreak on her once she crossed over. She may have felt she would be subjected to eternal damnation.

Even though there was a blueprint for the remainder of the farmhouse, she threw it away. It was then Mrs. Winchester began to not only design, but also oversee the construction of the house. If she wasn't guided by the spirits in the building of her house, then she no doubt relied on her collection of architectural and technical books, magazines, and engineering plans stored in the library next to her séance room. After the midnight séances, she supposedly conducted, the following day she or her niece gave that day's plans to her foreman, John Hansen. He made sure they were carried out to her specifications. Sometimes Mrs. Winchester would stroll the property with her foreman, checking on previously constructed features. Some of the plans were perplexing, yet they showed she had a definite talent for building. During these walks, she noticed that some of her plans didn't turn out as she had anticipated. Sarah would then order changes to be made by tearing it down, changing it in some manner, building around or over it, or completely ignoring the error, thus creating the bizarre features of the house. When this happened she would stop and use a sawhorse table to draw revised plans using the back of envelopes, or brown paper bags. Mr. Hansen probably never argued with her; since he was more concerned with the interpretation of the plans and how best to carry them out. The bizarreness of the house lies not in the construction methods, but through the individual features that are unique to her house.

At the beginning of construction, the eight-room farmhouse expanded quickly to 26 rooms within the span of six months. The outside of the house looks like an ordinary, if not oversized, sprawling Victorian mansion in the late Queen Anne style, vaguely Eastern in detail. Victorian architecture drew deeply from history, nature, geometry, theory, and personal inspiration to create the designs incorporated in the homes built between 1825-1900. Mrs. Winchester's house reflected the archetypal Victorian style in many ways. The house is decorated with a wide variety of architectural ornaments and an assortment of shingle types.

There are balconies, porches, cupolas, turrets, towers, pediments, witches' caps, curved walls, and an elaborate variety of windows. There is spindle work that includes clusters of wooden balls, jigsaw ornaments, trellises, and arches. There are also corbels, cartouches, and balustrades. Houses designed in the Victorian style used an array of wall materials, and the Winchester house is a perfect example of this. Incorporated into the design are horizontal wood siding, shingles of various shapes and sizes and vertical paneling. The roofs, save those that are flat metal decks, consist of a deep reddish hue of ridge cresting, and are adorned with finials, cornice work, and gables.

Sarah spared no expense in purchasing the finest of materials with which to construct the house. She used the highest grade of timber, some harvested from halfway across the world. Throughout her home, she incorporated various woods such as West African mahogany, boxwood, ash, rosewood, maple, redwood and ebony, to name a few.

Inside, the house is a virtual maze, as one might imagine from an overhead view of the mansion. There are miles of corridors with unusual twists and turns. Some of these corridors end in closets, others in blank walls. The halls themselves vary in widths ranging from two feet to regulation size. Some of the ceilings are so low that an average sized person has to stoop in order to prevent hitting their head.

There are 40 staircases with a total of 376 steps in the 24,000 square foot house. Some of these staircases lead to other rooms, one stops just inches below the ceiling, while yet another is a Y-shaped staircase where a person can reach three different levels of the home. Several stairways have steps only two inches high. One of these staircases is a switchback type; it has 44 steps that turn seven times, yet only rises nine feet. It was no doubt easier for Mrs. Winchester to climb these small stairs, thus easing her arthritis, than climbing the standard sized steps that were incorporated into the house.

The switchback stairs.

Therefore, it is not surprising her house has 3 elevators, particularly in view of her later years, when she used a wheelchair to help her get around. Two elevators were powered by water pressure, the other by electricity. They were the first fully automatic elevators on the West coast.

There are 950 doors and they are as diverse as the other architectural features. Most of them are made from mahogany; while others are redwood, painted to look like birds-eye maple. Other doors have leaded beveled glass installed, such as the double front doors. Others have plate glass, such as in the bathroom and conservatories. Doorknobs are made from copper or silver, carved with various designs. Door hinges consist of bronze or silver, the hinges in her bedroom are of gold. Not surprisingly, some of these doors open out, when they should open in and visa versa. The locks are just as bewildering; some locks are only on the outside, while some are only on the inside. One example, are the séance room doors that can only be opened while inside the room.

One of the doors is only 4 feet 10 inches high, just the right size for Mrs. Winchester's petite frame to pass through, while people of average height would hit their head. The door next to it however, is eight feet high. Other doors open onto blank walls, some onto a skylight frame with a two-story drop. The door in one of the bedrooms opens up to a fifteen-foot drop into the garden below. A cupboard opens up to ½" of storage space, while another opens to the 30 rooms beyond. The front entrance has double doors made from mahogany; and the key is made of gold. The four windowpanes in the doors contain rock quartz crystals made of beveled glass with a fleur de lis pattern set in a German leaded frame. On days when the sun shines through, the entrance hall sparkles as if on fire.

There are 1,257-framed windows, consisting of various styles, sizes, shapes, designs, and colors. In these frames a total of 10,000 glass panes are installed, more than are in the Empire State Building. Some windows consist of plate glass, such as the ones installed in the kitchens, skylights, the greenhouse cupolas, and the South Conservatory, a room Sarah used for her plants and flowers. Some windows use optical glass, either convex or concave, magnifying the view outside. Beveled glass is also used in some of the windows, including the double doors of the front entrance. Other windows have 13 blue and amber jewels embedded in a spider web pattern, while other spider web designed windows use only black leading, both conceived by Mrs. Winchester.

Spider web window in the 13th bathroom.

Even her favorite flower, the daisy, is integrated into stained glass windows of her design. They were manufactured in Austria, although probably ordered through Tiffany's of New York, as were many of the windows. The most expensive window in her home was made by Louis Comfort Tiffany, costing her $1,500, now it's considered priceless. The window consists of shades of violet, green, blue, and golden yellow on a clear background. It was designed to refract the sun's rays into rainbow prisms of light. Unfortunately, the window would never dazzle the eye with its multihued colors, having been installed in a Northern-facing wall. To make matters worse, another room was built behind it, making it impossible for the sunlight to reach it. These two faux pas made the window obsolete, leaving one to imagine the beautiful colors it would have emanated.

Her favorite bedroom, the Daisy bedroom, had long rectangular stained glass windows custom-made in Austria. The design consists of a tortoiseshell colored border, a daisy bush design in the lower half of the window and an oval window in the center magnifying the landscape outside. Larger daisies with their 13 petals are at the top of the window.

The daisy window.

A pair of stained glass windows in the Grand Ballroom is set on either side of the brick fireplace. These two rectangular windows have quotations from two Shakespearean plays. "Wide unclasp the table of their thoughts" is from *Troilus and Cressida*, spoken by Ulysses. It pertains to Cressida's flirtatious behavior. The other quotation "And these same thoughts people this little world" is from *Richard II* when he is talking to himself in his jail cell.

No one knows what significance these quotes had for Mrs. Winchester and why they were important enough for her to use in the two windows. Perhaps by quoting these two phrases within the context of their individual scenes, it can be determined what meaning she received from them. From *Troilus and Cressida* Ulysses says:

"Fie! Fie upon her!
There's language in her eye, her cheek, her lip,
Nay, her foot speaks: her wanton spirits look out
At every joint and motive of her body.
O' these encounters, so glib of tongue,
That give a coasting welcome ere it comes,
And wide unclasp the table of their thoughts
To every ticklish reader! Set them down
For sluttish spoils of opportunity,
And daughters of the game."

Shakespearean quote from *Troilus and Cressida*.

From *Richard II*, the full quote is as follows:

"I have studying how I may compare
This prison where I live unto the world:
And, for because the world is populous,
And here is not a creature but myself,
I cannot do it—yet I'll hammer it out.
My brain I'll prove the female to my soul,
My soul the father: and these two beget
A generation of still-breeding thoughts,
And these thoughts people this little world,
In humours like the people of this world,
For no thought is contented. The better sort,—
As thoughts of things divine, —are intermix'd
With scruples, and do set the word itself
Against the word:
As thus—Come, little ones: and then again,—
It is as hard to come as for a camel
To thread the postern of a needle's eye.
Thoughts tending to ambition, they do plot
Unlikely wonders: how these vain weak nails
May tear a passage through the flinty ribs
Of this hard world, my ragged prison walls;
And, for they cannot, died in their own pride.
Thoughts tending to content flatter themselves
That they are not the first of fortune's slaves,
Nor shall be the last; like silly beggars,
Who, sitting the stocks, refuge their shame,
That many have, and others must sit there;
And in this thought they find a kind of ease,
Bearing their own misfortunes on the back
Of such as have before endur'd the like.
Thus play I, in one person, many people,
And none contented: sometimes I am king,
Then treason makes me wish myself a beggar,
And so I am: then crushing penury
Persuades me I was better when a king:
Then I am king'd again: and by and by

Think that I am unking'd by Bolingbroke,
And straight am nothing:—but what'er I am,
Nor I, nor any man that but man is,
With nothing shall be pleas'd till he be eas'd
With being nothing. —Music do I hear?
(Music)
Ha, ha! Keep time: —how sour sweet music is
When time is broke and no proportion kept!
So, it is in the music of men's lives.
And here have I the daintiest of ear
To check time broke in a disorder'd string;
But, for the concord of my state and time,
Had not an ear to hear my true time broke.
I wasted time, and now doth time waste me;
For now hath time made me his numbering clock:
My thoughts are like minutes and, with sighs, they jar
Their watches on unto mine eyes, the outward watch,
Whereto my finger, like a dial's point,
Is pointing still, in cleansing them from tears.
Now, sir, the sound that tells what hours it is,
Are clamorous groans that strike upon my heart,
Which is the bell: so sighs, and tear, and groans,
Show minutes, times, and hours, —but my time
Runs posting on in Bolingbroke's proud joy,
While I stand fooling here, his Jack o'the clock.
This music mads me; let it sound no more;
For though it have holp madmen to their wits,
In me, it seems it will make wise men mad.
Yet blessing on his heart that gives it me!
For ' tis a sign of love; and love to Richard
Is a strange brooch in this all-hating world."

Shakespearean quote from "Richard II"

Perhaps Sarah and her husband, William, had attended these two plays in Connecticut. They may have been their favorite plays, speeches, or quotations, and was a reminder of happier times. On the other hand, she knew the ballroom was where she would entertain herself or others, possibly desiring a theme along those lines. Yet, they may have had a deeper meaning.

The speech from *Troilus and Cressida* could have reminded her of her days as a young belle in Connecticut and expressed the way she felt about those years. Perhaps others saw her in the same light when she was young.

She might have identified with Richard II's speech, feeling as if she were in her own personal prison, particularly, after losing her family, and being a widow in semi-seclusion. It was possible Sarah believed time was now wasting her and was unable to see the future, much like Richard II, whose situation had crept up on him. The same thought that Richard II had, that others suffered like her, could have comforted Mrs. Winchester.

Yet, another rationalization is that by putting the two quotes together they contained a distinct meaning for her. "Wide unclasp the table of their thoughts"; "These same thoughts people this little world" might have alluded to the spirits supplying her with her building instructions. By having séances every night, she may have felt she was opening the door to the thoughts and ideas of the spirits, and that in these thoughts, they took shape in the form of the rooms she built.

On the other hand, Mrs. Winchester, being a creative woman and ahead of her time, may have seen it as an invitation for people to open their minds, to free them of conventional thoughts and think imaginatively. She may have believed these unique thoughts "people this little world." It might be that she believed in the power of ideas. On the other hand, perhaps they had an even deeper meaning only she knew.

There are a total of 52 skylights, some built directly on top of each other; one rises four levels, while one looks into the kitchen below. Some interior skylights have never been exposed to the sun. One is installed in the floor of the sun porch with a railing around it, peering through it one can see the polished floor of the room below.

The floors of her mansion are made from various hardwoods, consisting of intricate and exquisite designs. Most floors are of inlaid parquetry using exotic woods in geometric patterns, such as squares, diamonds, and a herringbone pattern, among others. The Grand Ballroom, for example, is made from seven different woods—oak, maple, cherry, ash, teak, mahogany, and Mexican Rosewood. Men from New York installed the floor without using nails, an innovation at the time. The floor of her bedroom is constructed in a herringbone pattern; light and dark stripes can be seen the length of the floor when viewed at the proper angle. Some floors in her home required the work of one man for a single year. One craftsman worked 33 years for Sarah Winchester doing nothing but building and tearing up the flooring. She had linoleum installed in some of the kitchens and servants' quarters.

The ceilings and some of the walls are covered with French Lincrusta, made from pulverized wood and linseed oil. Some of the wallpaper used is a quarter of an inch thick; it was very expensive when originally purchased, costing $1.50 per square foot. One French Lincrusta wall covering is a rare scalloped shell design used in the front parlor. Wallpaper, most likely purchased in the United States, is also used throughout the house. Wood paneling of all widths and heights, are either stained to a glossy richness or painted in the color of her choice. Paneling is seen in the stairwells, bathrooms, kitchens as well as the séance room and the Grand Ballroom. Polished wood is used in the rooms she lived in, serviceable rooms such as kitchens and bathrooms were painted. Mrs. Winchester spared no expense in furnishing her house, purchasing from the East Coast, as well as the European countries of Germany, France, and Austria. She used exotic, expensive woods throughout the house in the fireplace mantels, parquetry floors, paneling, stairs, molding, and doors.

There is an oversized room containing built-in chests with deep drawers and bins, made by expert cabinetmakers. They used only the smoothest and most beautifully polished woods.

She used this storage area for her abundant stock of rare silks, satins, delicate Belgium pillow laces, as well as filet laces handmade in France and Italy. There were linens from Ireland, hand-embroidered in China and the Philippines and bolts of luxurious material shipped from India, Persia, and the far corners of the earth.

There are approximately 160 rooms in the mansion, 40 of these are bedrooms, thirteen bathrooms, six kitchens, two basements, two conservatories and one séance room. The house eventually spread over the Southeast section of the estate, encircling the outlying structures. This included the barn and hayloft that she incorporated as a part of her house, using the hayloft for storing items that were to be installed later in the house. These items included glazed tiles, Lincrusta wallpaper, fireplace mantels, doors, windows, and glass or crystal lamp shades among other items.

Sarah's favorite number, thirteen, abounded throughout the house and to a lesser extent on the grounds of her estate. Inside the house there are 13 windows in the 13th bathroom, 13 blue and amber jewels in a spider web window, 13 hooks in the séance room, 13 ceiling panels in the Guest Reception hall, and many more. At the end of the Carriage Entrance Hallway, there is a window with 13 panes of glass. There are four rows of 13 cement blocks in the Carriage Entrance Hall, 13 glass cupolas in the greenhouse, as well 13 California Fan Palms lining the carriage entrance. She also had a will with thirteen parts, which she signed thirteen times.

In ancient times, the number 13 was unlucky for evil persons. Giles de Rais, alias Bluebeard, was tried in France. There were 12 others tried with him to bring them all bad luck, and it did. There had also been 13 people at the Last Supper, with Judas as the thirteenth person. If she did believe the spiritualist, perhaps she used the number to deter evil spirits, as well as a method of protecting herself.

The most expensive room in the house was the Grand Ballroom built in 1900. There are very few nails in the hand-carved, elaborate woodwork, to improve the acoustics. On either side of the brick fireplace, there are two art glass windows, each decorated with a quote from two Shakespearean plays. In the middle of the room hung a German silver chandelier with thirteen candles encased by crystal shades. It originally had 12, but she had an electrician add one more. The elaborately carved wood ceiling panels have thirteen sub panels. Sarah Winchester contracted the construction of the room outside of her personal coterie of craftsmen. Construction on the room cost $9,000, which at that time was two to three times the cost of building the average home!

Every room had at least one door, if not two or three. This meant that each door had its own lock and with 950 doorways, there were enough keys to fill two water buckets. In these rooms, there are 47 fireplaces, with 17 chimneys; no two fireplaces are alike. The mantelpieces also vary, not only in design, but also in the materials used. They were hand carved, using such woods as mahogany, teak, oak, cherry, as well as marble. The material used for the fireplace fronts also varied. She used pipestone in the Front Hall, highly glazed Swedish tile in the Front Parlor and brick in the South Conservatory. The pillars carved from various woods are all installed upside down, supposedly to confuse the ghosts. There is even a fireplace on the sun porch, perhaps in order to help Mrs. Winchester with her arthritis. She utilized steam radiators, gas, and wood fireplaces, not to mention a coal furnace in the basement, supplementing the limited central heating of her home.

The bathrooms left little or no privacy for the occupant with their glass doors and windows. It was easy for someone to peer into as he or she walked through the hallways. Sarah had freestanding Swiss molded bathtubs, and toilets with a pull chain attached to the tank near the ceiling. Other bathrooms had washbowls with inlaid mosaic tiles. The thirteenth bathroom was the last one built and the one that Sarah used. There are 13 e-z riser steps leading into this last bathroom, with 13 windows displaying a spider web pattern a top long rectangular windows. In addition, one bathroom, containing just a sink and toilet, is only accessible from the outside door in the front yard. While this may seem strange, it was in actuality a logical idea. It was no doubt used by gardeners working on the grounds so they wouldn't track dirt into her home. They also had a convenient facility to use while they worked.

Mrs. Winchester even had a sewing room in which her clothing, drapes, and other household cloth items were made. It was said she would purchase entire bolts of cloth so no one else would have the same design.

Sarah also had an aviary for her tropical birds located across from the basement entrance. She kept the temperature carefully maintained using heat from the steam-producing furnace in the basement. It had a gravel floor and was accessible by both the house and the gardens.

Mrs. Winchester had two basements with wooden cupboards lining one wall, used for storing canned foods. One basement was easily accessible by a narrow staircase, as well as an elevator that took 15 seconds to get to each floor. In the front basement was a chute used to deliver the coal, adjacent to the furnace. The coal was then used to fire the furnace and several of the 47 fireplaces. Radiators installed on the basement ceiling, sent steam through the pipes of the house for warmth, and helped to heat the first floor.

In one location of the mansion, 10 feet by 28 feet, there are seven sources of heat, four fireplaces, and three forced-air furnace registers. Once the doors were closed, Mrs. Winchester turned up the heat to her liking, helping to ease her arthritis.

Of the bedrooms damaged in the Earthquake, had wallpaper made from crushed mica of a bluish green hue. When the sunlight hit the paper, it would sparkle, dazzling the eye.

The last bedroom she slept in, looked down on the side garden and a crescent shaped hedge, pointing directly to her bedroom. The herringbone-patterned floor in the room had alternating bands of dark and light when looking from the correct angle. There is a small dressing room at the back with a fireplace and a small bookcase. It was in this room Sarah died.

A person would expect the rooms of such a wealthy lady to be palatial, elaborate, and lavish, much in the same vein of

William Randolph Hearst's "San Simeon," or the famous Vanderbilt's summer home "Biltmore," such is not the case. The rooms are surprisingly small. Yet, when one considers she had few visitors and was the only inhabitant besides her niece and the necessary servants, it is easy to comprehend the reason for their smallness. Being a diminutive woman, she did not require a lot of room to move about in or to live in. Having few, if any visitors, it was not necessary for her to accommodate a large amount of people at any one time.

Sometimes there are two rooms built side by side with a few inches of space between their respective walls. Due to its construction, there are odd shaped, small shelves in a dressing room where it seems nothing much would fit. It might have been a small cupboard used for either books or knick-knacks. Some of these seem to be useless cubbyholes where nothing could be stored and may have been one of the mistakes she made in building her home.

Where the servants worked, the architecture is for the most part, utilitarian and simple. Walls were decorated by rounded or flat vertical paneling, and were painted instead of stained and highly polished, as was the remainder of the house. Shelves in the kitchens were plain, with no elaborate carvings; windows were of plate glass and the floors of linoleum. Tiles were used underneath one of the kitchen stoves to diffuse the heat from the wooden floor.

Mrs. Winchester had six kitchens in her home; the ones that were completed were used during various periods throughout her residency. One kitchen, used before the earthquake of 1906 had been damaged, and two unfinished kitchens were boarded up after the 1906 quake. There were two kitchens for the servants, one on the third floor, and one near the Venetian dining room. There was always one working kitchen for Mrs. Winchester and one for the servants.

The rooms that Sarah Winchester inhabited were more decorative and elaborate. The floors were usually of inlaid parquetry in geometric designs and were highly polished. Windows consisted of oval, diamond, square, rectangular or round designs. Some held stained glass, mullioned glass, and convex or concave glass, the latter magnifying the view outside her living quarters. Fireplaces consisted of fine imported woods and glazed tiles or brick. The woods used for paneling, floors, trims, doors and stairs were usually of a rich, dark hue or honey tone that were highly polished. Floral and geometric patterns were used in the Lincrusta wallpaper that covering some walls and ceilings; she also incorporated French wallpaper of various designs.

The architectural elements were not gaudy or ostentatious. There was nothing of the rococo or baroque style in the decorations. Patterns, while elaborate, were usually of a floral or botanical motif. Perhaps her East Coast upbringing influenced the design of the home's architecture as well as the period in which it was built. The designs used throughout the home are elaborate, yet refined, elegant, and to some extent, puritanical. There were no loud colors clashing on the wallpaper or Lincrusta, and while intricate at times, for the most part, the walls were either white or subdued colors with clean, uncluttered patterns. Some of the paneling in her living quarters was quite dark, for example, the Venetian dining room, or of a honey tone, as in the Grand Ballroom.

The house itself was a maze with unexpected twist and turns; stairs would lead to the ceiling, corridors would lead to dead ends, stairs would make several turns, yet rise only nine feet, doors would open onto blank walls or to the back 30 rooms of the mansion. There is a window as one descends a flight of stairs, that looks into a elevator shaft. One balcony that is three feet deep, narrows to 3 inches, doors open in when they should open out, some have locks only on the outside of the door. Despite its bizarre features it is an elegant, refined house, decorated in the best of taste.

The Garden and Orchard

The gardens, being no different from the house, echoed the design of the mansion. It had its own twists and turns of pathways winding their way around the mansion, straight paths, intertwining ones, and those that lead nowhere.

The first job Mrs. Winchester gave her full-time staff of eight gardeners, was planting a cypress hedge around the property. It was to eventually shield the house from passersby and give the resident a sense of privacy. It was said that at one time, the hedge grew so tall, only the top floor of the mansion could be seen from the road.

The garden was as lush as the interior of the house was elegant. In some ways, it was designed like a typical Victorian garden with its use of geometric designs and neatly trimmed shrubs. Sarah, an avid gardener, was proud of the beautiful surroundings she created. While the garden was bordered by 14,000 rare dwarf boxwood hedges, acres of blooming flower beds abounded, and a variety of trees and shrubs were imported from over 110 countries. Walking around the park-like grounds, one could view the various trees the gardeners had planted. There were Peruvian pepper, European black loquat, English yew, catalpa, monkey puzzle tree, English walnut, elm, pink crepe myrtle, Bayleaf tree, Norfolk, and Spanish pine. She also planted individual fruit and citrus trees such as persimmon, orange, lemon, and grapefruit. There were various species of palms on the property, including Canary Date palms and the 13 California Fan palms lining the carriage drive to her home. Included in her assortment of ornamental shrubs was pampas grass, roses, India Hawthorne, star jasmine, hydrangea, lilies and her favorite flower, the daisy. Vines of all kinds, including Boston ivy were used. Outside her bedroom was a crescent shaped boxwood hedge that some say held a spiritualistic meaning for her.

Like most Victorian gardens of the time, not only were there ornamental flowers and shrubs, but also plants grown for medicinal purposes. The fruits of the sourberry supposedly purified the blood, persimmons were used for intestinal disorders, while peonies were used to cure headaches and parts of the rose plants were used as an eye lotion for medicinal purposes.

Even though Mrs. Winchester had her own ideas for her garden, she used several horticultural books for reference, much as she used her architectural books to construct the house. She relied on *Vick's Flower and Garden, The California Vegetable Garden and Field* by Edward J. Wickson, as well as a book by A. J. Dowling, published in 1841, still a popular book at the turn of the century. Her head gardener, "Tommy" Nishiwara made certain the hedge and gardens were maintained.

The garden, separated by circuitous pathways, winded past several handcrafted European lead statues in various forms. Displaying the ancient classics, in statues and fountain pieces, was a typical feature of Victorian homes. Some of the statues are freestanding; others are integrated into the Victorian fountains on her grounds. One of the two life-size statues near the front entrance is Demeter, the Greek goddess of agriculture. This seems appropriate when taking into consideration her interest in her gardens and orchard.

The life-size statue which people considered unusual, was Native American, "Chief Little Fawn," holding a bow and broken arrow. Some people said the lawn statue was meant to placate the Indians killed by the Winchester rifle. However, this type of statue was typical of the times, and if the gossipers had paid attention to detail, they would have noticed the Indian statue was poised diagonally across from the life size statue of a deer.

The other statues were integrated into four separate fountains. One has an egret spouting water; the second, made by J. L. Mott Company of New York, has a serpent consisting of corrosion resistant metal, zinc and tin. The third has both a cupid and a swan, with frogs emitting a water spray around the edge. The fourth fountain has a cherub riding a mythological sea monster called a hippocampus, (a combination of a horse's head and a fish's body). Originally, all the fountains had brick foundations coated with several layers of rough concrete.

On the estate, Sarah has a greenhouse with 13 glass cupolas where her gardeners cultivated and tended to her plants. These plants and flowers were brought inside to brighten and decorate her home. Later they were returned to the greenhouse and continued to be cared for, until they were used again.

Mrs. Winchester loved spending time in her garden. She had four gazebos built, enabling her to relax in comfort, while enjoying the lush landscape surrounding her. The gazebos were situated in various spots around the grounds.

The front gate of wrought iron, leading to the main entrance of the house, consisted of a rainbow and sun design, which only Sarah Winchester knew its significance. Attaching the gates were two sandstone pillars. They came from a stone quarry in Alameda, the same quarry used for the stones of Stanford University in Palo Alto. Words were carved on the front of each gatepost. On one post was her name, "S. L. Winchester," on the other, was the name she gave her house, "Llanda Villa." Many people have come up with several interpretations of the name. In Spanish, it means, "house on flat land," another possible translation given was "my plain little house." The word "llano" in Spanish means, "plane," as in flat. The word "villa" means "town" in Spanish. If referring to the Latin version, it means "row of houses." Yet, in today's context it has come to mean a country estate, a rural suburban residence of a wealthy person, or an agricultural estate of either Ancient Rome or early medieval times. This would be a perfect interpretation because it was a rural, suburban residence of a very wealthy person. It was also an agricultural estate since she had 141 acres of orchards. If "Llanda" means flat, then it makes perfect sense because the house is built on flat land. It has also been said to mean "my plain little house." While not exactly plain, it was not ostentatious in the rococo or baroque style of design. In checking a Spanish dictionary a word that comes close to, "Llanda" is "llantos" which means weeping. This name would also be appropriate since she had lost her husband and child, reflecting her situation.

She kept herself busy not only with 18 acres of gardens, but also with her orchards, covering 141 acres of the total 161 acres she owned. It was there she had apricot, walnut, and plum trees. She retained ten field hands year round to work in the orchard. When it was time to harvest the crops she hired an additional 10 to 15 workers.

The plums in her orchard were the most labor intensive of her crops. Once the workers picked the plums, they boxed them in the field, before being taken to the dehydrator. The dehydrator was located in the fruit-drying shed where the plums were turned into prunes. First, workers sorted out the plums on a wooden table, dropping the bad ones into a shoot. Then they were set in lye water in order to break the skin so they would dry faster. They were then put on trays, 20 pounds per tray, with 160 trays per load. Underneath the racks, a wood-burning furnace was heated to 200 degrees. The racks were then rotated several times and the prunes turned so they would dry faster. The workers used a crank for loading and rotating the trays, drying one and a half tones of prunes in 30 hours. The fruit was put in wooden boxes with the name S. L. Winchester stenciled in black lettering. She sold her fruit at local markets, across the country, and even across the ocean to Europe and England, supplementing her income. Her orchard was listed in the early San Jose city directories under fruit growers.

On her grounds, there was a freestanding bell tower. As construction continued, the house snaked around it until it was practically enclosed in its twisted path. This bell tower has smooth interior walls with the rope dangling down inside, and is accessible from outside her bedroom. The bell ringer telephoned an astronomical observatory in order to check the accuracy of his chronometers, the best that money could afford. He also used an expensive watch setting it and the chronometers to the correct time.

According to the local grapevine, the neighbors heard the bell toll at midnight, as well as one and two o'clock in the morning. The midnight ringing was allegedly used to call the spirits to her séances. The second and third ringing of the bells was to send the spirits back to their resting places. Whatever the purpose, the tolling bells served late at night; it was used to send the workers to the orchards, to call them in for meals and call them in at the end of the day. It was also used as a fire alarm.

The bell tower.

On her grounds was a 35-foot water tower with a 10,000-gallon water tank for storage, thus serving as the main water supply for the estate. There are miles of drainpipe running through the house, allowing the water to run into several collection basins. The water is then carried to several cisterns scattered around the grounds. The bottom half of the tower was used as a plumber's workshop, where repairs could be done, while the upper floors were utilized as the field hands' living quarters. A carpenters' workshop was on the premises as well, where pillars and ornamental woodwork Sarah commissioned for her home, could be carved by her own craftsmen.

Mrs. Winchester also had her own gas manufacturing plant. It was used to press gas through the lines of the house and to ignite the gaslights in her home. In the pump house, a Pierce gas engine provided the electricity used to operate the Otis elevator, along with several well pumps.

Before the advent of the automobile, Sarah Winchester used the stable to accommodate the horses that pulled her Victoria carriage. She had a garage built after purchasing her first automobile for $8,400. It was a 1909 French Renault with a battery operated starter. She then purchased a 1917 Pierce Arrow Limousine, paying $7,200 at the time, painted lavender with gold trim. At the time of her death, it was worth $1,500. She also owned a 1916 Buick truck used for inspecting the estate. During this time, she not only had a garage, where repairs on her automobiles were carried out, but on the other side of the wall was a carwash, enabling her to keep her car clean.

Mrs. Winchester's estate was virtually self-sufficient. This was most likely done on purpose, given the fact that she was so far from the town's stores that supplied her with household necessities. Having her own water supply, gas plant, pump house and well pumps, she never had any utility bills. With plumber and carpenters' workshops, she had no need to contract outside work that could be done just as easily on the premises. The stable, garage, and car wash, enabled her to maintain and repair her various modes of transportation. Her orchard, herb, and vegetable garden were undoubtedly for her own personal use, as well as for profit, as were the cow and chickens she raised. She needed very few purchases outside her property with the exception of fabric, household items, and clothes, though curtains, drapes, and upholstery items were made in the sewing room. It was a well-run, efficient home, all overseen by Mrs. Winchester.

Innovations

Mrs. Winchester, a lady who was definitely ahead of her time, owned and used many new fangled inventions. Perhaps she wanted to be "first on the block," so to speak, or maybe to make her life easier by managing tasks more efficiently. Her wealth also helped her to purchase new inventions that the ordinary person could not afford; particularly in what was then, a rural community. The up-to-date conveniences used were both inside and outside her home.

Inside the home, decorated brass corner plates were installed at the sides of each stair step to keep dust from collecting in the corners, making cleaning of the stairs easier.

Some of the windows have specially designed catches used to close and open the window that are patterned after a Winchester rifle trigger and trip hammer. An inside crank was used to open and close outside window shutters. It was an innovation that later became common in people's homes.

Mrs. Winchester had several modern innovations to assist in heating her mansion. One source of heat came from steam radiators, some attached to the ceiling of the basement to heat the floor above. A coal chute located in the front basement, allowed coal to be dumped adjacent to the boiler, it was used to heat the water, making steam for the radiators. Steam was then forced through miles of pipe running throughout the house, anything that cooled down before being released, was sent back to the boiler to be reheated. Radiators attached to the basement ceiling, heated the first floor for efficiency. Sand was deposited between floor studs, giving the floor excellent insulation, as well as acoustical effects between the floors.

She no doubt used the multitude of windows and skylights as a method of heating. The windows would let the sun in warming the home, no doubt helping to ease her arthritis. Some skylights had wooden slats installed several feet below it, between the vertical walls, with the narrow edge upwards. This served a dual purpose; one was to let in a degree of filtered light to the rooms below. The second purpose enabled the servants to lay boards across these slats, where they would stand and wash the outside windows of the rooms. It was a very ingenious way to keep the outer windows clean.

Sarah Winchester applied simple methods to obtain access to her maze of a house. The first were three elevators; two run by hydraulics, the other, an Otis elevator, was run by electricity. The Otis elevator is the only feature in the house with a blueprint drawn for its construction. It took 10-15 seconds to get to each floor, enabling her servants to get down to the basement where the food was stored. Mrs. Winchester used them to facilitate her movement about the house when she had arthritis and needed a wheelchair to get around.

Electric Otis elevator motor.

Sarah had staircases built to make it easier or quicker for her to get around. There were several flights of stairs that had 2-inch risers; making it easier for her to climb them with her arthritis. One of these staircases makes 7 turns and has 44 steps, but rises only nine feet. There is also a staircase built in the shape of a "Y," allowing servants to get to their destination quicker. This staircase has three levels, one set of stairs starts on the first floor at the back porch steps. The second set starts on the second floor, where the linen rooms are located. The third set, also on the second floor, is located by the oriental bedrooms. Due to the construction methods, the second floor is not at the same level, there is a three-foot difference overall. Therefore, the staircase located near the oriental bedrooms is lower than the staircase in the linen rooms. If a servant started on the first floor they could go up to the landing, and chose to go either to the linen rooms or to the oriental bedrooms. If a servant was coming from the oriental bedroom, they could go down to the landing and from there, go up to the linen rooms or down to the first floor. A servant could go down seven stairs of one staircase, but have to take eleven stairs to get to the same place from the linen rooms. It may be confusing, but this is one of the oddities of the house.

The 7-11 stairs.

In order to communicate with the 18-20 domestic servants she employed, she used a call box or annunciator. She would push a button to signal the particular servant she wanted. A numbered card with would drop down in one of the windows, letting the servants know what room she was in. After she got their attention, she could speak with them through a series of voice tubes connected to the rooms.

Servants call box.

In one of the kitchens is an ornamental, cast-iron Jewel Company stove that used gas for cooking. Behind it, a storage tank was horizontally installed. The water tank, containing coils, heated the water for the house. The gas used for the stove was manufactured on the premises by a tank mixing air and high-octane gas.

In the kitchen, used after the 1906 Earthquake, the sinks are made of hand-carved soapstone with 13 holes in the drain covers. Another improvement is a hinged drain board, laminated and corrugated. In one of the kitchens, resembling an early day cash register is a char-broiler she used for cooking.

The laundry basins her servants used were made from a single piece of porcelain. The tools needed to do the wash, are a part of the sink. Both the soap tray above, and the scrub board below, are molded into the porcelain, making a metal or wood scrub board obsolete. It was said Sarah Winchester held a patent for this laundry sink, however, the patent has never been found.

The only shower in the house was for her use alone, and was located in the 13th bathroom, the last one built. She designed this shower specifically for her height, so it would spray her body and not her hair. The water, thermostatically controlled, had a needle-spray coming from an upside down u-shaped brass tube.

The conservatory where she kept her plants have sloped floors with removable wood panels. The panels were removed before the plants were watered, exposing a zinc sub-floor. With this innovation, the wood floors would not be ruined. Any overflow from the plants trickled down the sloping floor, where the pipes were located, then continued through them, to the garden below. There is an elaborate drainage system, starting with miles of drainpipe, running through the house ending up in several collection basins around the yard. The water was then carried to cisterns located around the grounds for holding the water. There are water pipes emerging beneath second story windows, meant to be used in conjunction with window boxes that were never installed.

Sarah Winchester's gas manufacturing plant produced carbide gas for her home. It consisted of a water tank with a floater resting on the water's surface. When the floater reached a certain water level, calcium carbide tablets were released into the water below, producing carbide gas in the tank. It was then pressed through the gas lines of the house by a large piston and pin cylinder. This allowed the gaslights of the house to be lit by electro-mechanical strikers or buttons, creating a spark to light each lamp. The gas pump fueled an electric generator that was used in lighting the house, providing the electricity for several well pumps, and the Otis elevator. The gas was both colorless and odorless, so if it had been leaking, it would have gone undetected. This could have been very dangerous, since it was highly flammable. Had it exploded, it could have killed people, which, surprisingly enough, it never did.

In order to slow down any possible fires, she used steel lathe in some of the walls. This metal lathe was used in the carwash and some of the walls in the Daisy bedroom. Sand was also used to insulate the floors of the Daisy bedroom for the same purpose. Should the flames burn through the floor the sand would fall on the fire below to smother it.

The 10,000-gallon water storage tank was the main source of water on the estate, thus making her self-sufficient in this respect. It was used for the house, gardens, and the carwash. When Sarah Winchester acquired her cars, attached to the opposite side of the garage was a car wash. In it there was a wood stove on one side of the room and a freestanding water heater beside it. In the ceiling, there was a 360-degree rotating pipe; a hose was attached to spray the heated water over the entire car, something no one else had in Santa Clara County.

These innovations and new technological inventions were not common to most homes in America. Most people did not have indoor plumbing, or indoor bathrooms, much less charbroilers or carwashes. She not only had the funds, but the imagination to use these new inventions for her own purposes and needs. It was obvious she was not afraid to use the latest inventions. It made her house more efficient and made life easier as well.

The Death of Mrs. Winchester

On the morning of September 5, 1922, Mrs. Winchester died from heart failure while in her sleep. She was approximately 83 years old, her birth certificate having been burned in a Connecticut fire. The workers, hearing of her death, ceased construction, leaving nails half-driven into the wood, and rooms left unfinished. It was said that she spent $40,000,000 on the house, leaving only $4,000,000 remaining in her estate. In actuality, there was $2.9 million left at the time of her death.

Mrs. Winchester's
bedroom.

Several people who knew Sarah Winchester personally vouched for her sanity, as previously mentioned. Such declarations are from people who knew her. These first hand accounts prove a more valuable testimony to her true mental state, than the gossip of the local populace and legends that have sprung up from such talk.

Someone who was mentally unbalanced would never have written such a thorough, well thought out will. It was written on March 23, 1920, two and a half years before her death. It was twelve pages long, consisting of thirteen parts. Her personal physician Dr. Clyde Wayland witnessed it, as did attorneys Roy F. Lieb and S. F. Lieb.

The first part of her will instructed all her debts and funeral expenses be paid from her estate before anything else was done. She then bequeathed $3,000 to the trustees of the Evergreen Cemetery in New Haven, Connecticut, where she was buried alongside her husband and child. This trust fund was to insure the perpetual care of her cemetery lot, as well as the tombstone and copings. The trust fund was implemented to keep the lot "as beautiful as possible, as well as free of weeds and other undesirable growth." No one else was to be interred in her plot without her permission.

She then gave specific amounts of money to employees still on her payroll at the time of her death. She gave her foreman John Hansen, who lived on her estate with his family, $2,000. James Bogie, one of her gardeners, was also given $2,000. Henrietta Sivera, her maid and companion, received $3,000. Her Japanese maid, Misa Hirata received $2,000 and $500 was left to her head gardener, "Tommy" Nishiwara.

She also left money to her favorite charities, first to the Visiting Nurses' Association, which received $4,000 and $3,000 to the Home for the Friendless, both in New Haven, Connecticut.

In her will, she had the inheritance tax paid, before her gifts of money were given to her beneficiaries. She gave $3,000 outright to her sister, Mrs. Isabel Campbell Merriman, and the same amount to her niece, Marian Isabel Marriott. She gave $2,000 to her three nieces, Mrs. Sarah Louise Ruthrauff, Mrs.

Sarah Catherine McLean and Miss Louise Beecher Pardee and $1,000 to her grandniece Mrs. Mary Davis Marsh Proust.

Mrs. Winchester then had a specific amount of money set in separate trust funds to be safely invested. The net income from these funds paid her relatives in equal monthly payments throughout their lifetime. After their death, the remaining money from their individual trust funds would revert to the General Hospital Society of Connecticut.

In these trust funds, she bequeathed $200,000 both to her niece, Marian Isabel Marriott and to her sister, Mrs. Isabel Merriman. She left trust funds of $50,000 apiece to her nephews William Winchester Merriman, George Leonard Gerard, and William Pardee Sprague as well as to her nieces, Mrs. Sarah Louise Ruthrauff, Miss Louise Beecher Pardee, and Mrs. Sarah Catherine Mc Lean. To her nephew, Goldwin Smith Spencer she bequeathed trust funds of $40,000 and $30,000 to her nephew Charles Homer Sprague. Her grand nieces, Margaret Marriott, the adopted daughter of Marian Marriott, Anita McLean, and Mrs. Mary Davis Marsh Proust received $18,000 trust funds as well. Great grand nephews, William Marsh, and Bryant Marsh, (sometimes known as Risley), both sons of Mrs. Mary Davis Marsh Proust, received trust funds of $8,000 each.

She gave her sister and her favorite niece, Marian Marriott, the homes in Palo Alto, California where they lived. Sarah left all her furnishings, pictures, household goods, jewelry, and paraphernalia to Marian Marriott to do as she wished.

After all the gifts were given, if there was anything left of her estate, she instructed the Union Trust Company to keep 200/858 of the principal of the "said remainder" safely invested in a trust fund. The net income from the respective trusts to her sister, Isabel, and daughter, Marian was to be paid during their lifetime in equal monthly installments. Afterwards, she gave 50/858 of the principal on the remainder of her estate, to William W. Merriman, George L. Gerard, William P. Sprague, Sarah C. McLean, and Sarah L. Ruthrauff respectively. She bequeathed 40/858 to Goldwin S. Sprague, 18/858 apiece to Margaret Marriott, Hazel Beecher, Anita McLean, and Mary Davis Marsh Proust. She gave 30/858 to Charles H. Sprague and Louise B. Pardee, and 8/858 each to Bryant Marsh and William Marsh. These fractions were proportionate with the money allocated to her relatives in the first portion of her will.

The excess funds from the individual trusts were to be used to help further the "best interests" of the William Wirt Winchester Annex. They were to be utilized to give the "best possible care and treatment" to the tuberculosis patients who at or after her death, had been admitted into that part of the hospital.

Whatever else remained of her estate that had not been bequeathed was to be sold, including any property she owned at the time. The Union Trust Company of San Francisco was to handle this portion of her will, and was designated to hold the money in trust, investing it for all her relatives.

Marian Marriott decided to have her aunt's belongings auctioned off. When the contents were being removed from the house, it was only three-quarters furnished. It took six trucks, working six weeks for eight hours a day, to remove her possessions. One reason for taking so long, was the movers got lost while going through one-way doors, discovering they had reached a dead-end or finding themselves where they had started. When her belongings were being removed from the house, the $30,000 gold-plated dinner service she supposedly ate her meals on was not found. Instead, they discovered what was no doubt even more precious to Sarah Winchester. In the safe, they found fishing line, socks, woolen long underwear, newspaper clippings, and a tiny purple velvet box. In this box was a lock of her daughter's hair and the New Haven newspaper clipping of her daughter's obituary that read: "Winchester, In this city. July 24, 1866. Annie Pardee Winchester, infant daughter of William Wirt and Sarah L. Winchester." The remainders of her personal effects were then auctioned off in San Francisco. No record of the auction was kept, so her possessions have never been recovered.

Her mansion and farm were not mentioned in her will, perhaps because she thought no one would ever want such a huge, unique home or the labor intensive work that went with her 141 acres of orchards and 18 acres of gardens. This left her 160-room mansion and farm in the hands of the trust company. Her trustees sold the estate to locals a year after her death. The house that she had spent approximately $5.5 million to build, sold in 1923 for $135,531.10, a bargain price in the early 1920s. It was known for a time as "Winchester Park" where the residents of Santa Clara Valley held parties and picnics on the grounds and has been open to the public ever since. Years later they charged admission to the house. Now a popular tourist attraction, it has drawn people from all over the world to see the inscrutable Mrs. Winchester's mysterious mansion.

Restoration

After her death, the mansion was not maintained as it should have been. Therefore, it was necessary to do restoration on the house. Much like the non-stop building that occurred during her life, continuous work is being done on the refurbishment of the house. Employed for the jobs are carpenters, painters, and gardeners, some are the sons and grandsons of her original employees.

Restoration of the mansion is time consuming as well as painstaking. Curved shingles had to be hand cut before they could be nailed on a turret. All the doors and windows were specially shaped and angled, there was no square corner in the house as one might expect.

One room takes months to be done to perfection. The Victorian fixtures, moldings and hardware, as well as other materials, were specially ordered or manufactured on the spot in order to match the originals. Eventually almost everything will be restored, though part of the home remains as the 1906 Earthquake left it, with cracked plaster, torn wallpaper and wooden lathes exposed.

Because her original furnishings were auctioned off and never recovered, period pieces have been used to decorate her home. They have either been donated to or purchased by the Winchester Mystery House to give the tourist an idea of what the house looked like while she lived there.

The William Wirt Winchester Clinic

The William Wirt Winchester clinic still exists today, as does the Winchester Mystery House. It was originally named the William Wirt Winchester Hospital, his wife establishing a fund in 1909 under his name. Land for the hospital site was on Campbell Ave. in West Haven, Connecticut and was dedicated to the care of tuberculosis patients. Constructed in 1916, it was in operation from 1918-1946. Before its completion, the U.S. government leased the building for use as a military hospital until 1927. It operated as the Tuberculosis Division of New Haven Hospital from 1928-1940, eventually discontinuing its operation due to the decrease in tuberculosis cases. In 1948, the building and property were sold to the government. The name was then transferred to the Hospital's Private Pavilion in order to perpetuate the memorial. Now the fund continues to help patients with respiratory diseases at Yale-New Haven Hospital.

Conclusion

Rumors have abounded during and after Mrs. Winchester's lifetime, making it difficult to separate fact from fiction. The myths have been repeated so often they have become an accepted, if not erroneous, part of the story. Thus, there may not be as much mystery in Mrs. Winchester's life and mansion as there seems.

There are possible explanations for much of this misinformation. People might have invented incredible tall tales, searching for answers as to why she built the house in a helter-skelter manner. A simple question from someone on the subject, might have prompted the casual response, "She builds as the spirit moves her." This remark, joking or not, could have prompted tales of ghosts, spirits and curses, whether they were validated or not.

Whether Mrs. Winchester believed Boston Spiritualist Adam Coons, no one knows. She purportedly visited him, hoping to discover the reasons behind her husband's and daughter's deaths. The spiritualist told her the people who had been killed by the Winchester repeating rifle were responsible for her loved ones' deaths. If she didn't want the spirits to kill her or those she loved, she was to build continuously on a house. It is reported that Mr. Coons told her to move west; some dispute this part of the story. If she believed him, then perhaps she moved to California, where the availability of land was ample enough to build ceaselessly. This could be one explanation for moving to the West Coast and building the maze-like house. Perhaps she visited him to see if she could contact her deceased family, seeking advice or approval for her premeditated move from Connecticut

There is another story that physicians and friends in Connecticut suggested she seek a milder climate, perhaps to ease her arthritis. One doctor did tell her she should build a house without using an architect, the objective was to help her deal with her loss. Sarah could very well have considered their advice. Perhaps it was a combination of the two that convinced her to move.

The most commonly told story about Sarah Winchester is that she relied on nightly séances for her building plans. If this is true, it could account for the house's peculiarities. Assuming she held these séances, inferred she believed in an afterlife. It is possible Mrs. Winchester could have been trying to contact her deceased husband and daughter, instead of the spirits. Perhaps she was trying to contact both.

Rarely reported is that Mrs. Winchester referred to architectural, technical and reference books and magazines stored in her library. She used them to assist her in the construction of her mansion, referring to them as needed. Her architectural inexperience could have affected the design of the house. If a plan didn't work out as intended, she dealt with the problem in various ways. She would either have the structure torn out, built around, or completely ignored. This is evidenced by some of the house's oddities such as a cupboard with ¼" storage space, stairs that stop inches below the ceiling, corridors leading to dead ends and wrought iron bars on inside windows. Through a window on one of the stairway landings, one can view an elevator shaft. Other explanations could be that she simply changed her mind on a whim, deciding not to go through with a specific plan. She could have suddenly decided she needed a specific room built and found it conflicted with rooms already constructed. On the other hand, Mrs. Winchester might have considered her young nieces and nephews visiting her, by planning a maze they would enjoy exploring.

The stairs to nowhere.

Planning the construction spontaneously might have served as a diversion, keeping her mind off her loneliness and the death of her family. Architecture, much like reading or gardening, was another one of her interests. In constructing an immense house, she was also able to surround herself with people, to keep her from getting lonely.

Living by herself, except for servants, people must have wondered why she built such an enormous house. Her attorney Roy F. Lieb said she built it in the hopes her relatives from the East would visit her. However, of her relatives, none but her sister Isabel Merriman and her daughter Marian Marriott ever entered her home. The only relative to come from the East coast to her home was a nephew checking on his aunt's health. He never saw his aunt, however, since he was sent away with a check, delivered on a silver tray by her maid.

While the house she built was massive, the rooms themselves were not. They were rather small, cozy, and comfortable. Since Sarah was a petite person living alone, and unable to entertain, she didn't require spacious rooms to live in. Having large rooms might have made her feel alone, emphasizing the emptiness of the house.

The house, known for its many strange individual features, have some repetitive themes throughout the estate. One theme is the upside down columns or pillars used in the front porch, the fireplaces, and staircases. According to legend, it is said she had the columns installed this way to confuse evil spirits. If she followed the psychic's advice, this would resolve the question for the upside down columns.

Another possible explanation is that they held symbolic meaning, reflecting Sarah's perspective on her world. The upside down columns might represent how her life had been turned upside down, due to the death of her husband and daughter. It may have been a reminder or a mournful tribute, letting her departed loved ones know they were not forgotten. She may have had a wry sense of humor about her situation, thinking that something in her house should be upside down besides her life.

Much along the same lines is the various times the number thirteen arises on her estate. She planted 13 California fan palms lining the carriage driveway. There are 13 cement blocks in the carriage entrance hall, 13 glass cupolas on the roof of the greenhouse, 13 windows in the 13th bathroom. There are 13 wood fireplaces, 13 drain holes in a sink, 13 panes of glass in some of the windows, 13 petals on each daisy in the windows of her Daisy bedroom, and more.

The number thirteen, normally considered unlucky, was a number to be avoided at all costs if you were superstitious. If Mrs. Winchester subscribed to this fallacy, believing the medium's reading, then she used this number to keep evil spirits at bay. It's a possibility the places where Sarah inhabited the estate, the number thirteen occurred, the Grand Ballroom, the Guest

Hallway, the 13th bathroom, the greenhouse, the carriage house, among others. No one has done research to discover if the number 13, in some form, is in every room, or only in places she would pass through or in which she resided. With the mansion having 160 rooms, it would be a nearly impossible task.

If she was not superstitious, or did not believe the unlucky number would deter evil spirits; there could be other reasons she used the number. It might have been her way of flaunting superstition, as well as her fate, daring the number to bring her bad luck. After all what could be unluckier than losing your family? Perhaps she felt that surrounding herself with the number thirteen was a reminder of her misfortune. Some people have no superstitious fear, some even consider it their lucky number, and the number thirteen could have been hers.

Another repetitious symbol in her home was the spider web pattern, used in various windows. They include the upper square windows in the 13th bathroom, rectangular windows containing 13 blue and amber jewels, as well as oval windows. She was obviously fascinated by spiders and their webs, perhaps seeing beauty in their design. It was possible she identified with the arachnids for they were their own architects, building without a blue print, much like herself.

Her house, while considered bizarre, is definitely innovative and creative in its design. As the saying goes, "Necessity is the mother of invention," something that could be said for Mrs. Winchester's home. For a woman supposedly crazy, with a house full of peculiarities, there was logic behind some of the architectural features. One example is the 52 skylights used in both the house and the greenhouse. Most of the house's skylights are located far from the outer walls, where sunlight would normally enter. No doubt, they were installed for multi-purposes, one to let in more light to the inner recesses of the dark house. The other, to heat the rooms that the sunlight otherwise, would never reach. In essence, a primitive form of solar heating to help relieve her arthritis.

The famous stories that she spied on her servants through these skylights, for fear they were poisoning her are untrue. She would not have given them gifts of money, real estate or let them live on her estate rent free had she believed this. She also would not have signed her Christmas cards "Aunt Sadie." It is a telling signature that expressed her relationship with her servants. If she did spy on them, it was because she was making certain they were working. She did not tolerate laziness, gossip, revealed confidences, or theft, as told by an employee's son. Paying them twice the normal rate, she no doubt expected her employees to work hard and to be loyal.

Sarah had been reported to have trap doors in her home. In actuality, these were nothing more than removable wooden floor sections, located in the conservatory. They were removed when the plants were watered.

The two-inch high e-z risers served a logical purpose. Mrs. Winchester's body was in later years assailed by arthritis, affecting her extremities. It was difficult for her to get around in her later years, and using the smaller stairs made it easier for her. A woman, who was allegedly crazy, would not have had such a meticulous attention to detail and efficiency. The construction workers merely carried out her plans, she designed them.

Rumors of her wearing a veil everywhere she went, even inside her home, are completely unfounded. Wearing a veil inside the house would be pointless, as well as uncomfortably hot in summer. No purpose would be served by wearing a veil merely to hide her face from her employees, her sister, and niece, the latter knowing what she looked like any way. Supposedly, she wore the veil outside her home as well, yet the most telling evidence is the one photo taken in front of the house. She is sitting in a carriage, wearing a hat, her face clearly without a veil. Had she constantly worn a veil, she would have worn one in the photo.

It is untrue this very same photo is the only photo taken of her. There is a photo taken of her in a San Francisco photo studio at 124 Post Street, and another photo taken in the 1860s that is know to exist. Allegedly, it was taken without her knowledge by a gardener hiding behind a bush. This photo was not taken surreptitiously, as explained previously in an earlier chapter.

Talk of her being a recluse may merely have been a matter of perception. In those days, well-to-do widows were expected to remain in mourning for the remainder of their lives. This meant she was unable to entertain at home or socialize outside of it. Mrs. Winchester did go shopping for the household items she needed. She visited new neighbors or ailing people, bringing them food. She gave to charities as well, donating clothes. Other than that, she did not go to social events or entertain many guests in her home.

In her later years, her debilitating arthritis made it difficult for her to get around, one possible reason why she never emerged from her carriage while shopping. Merchandise was brought out to her instead. Eventually she needed a wheelchair to get around the house. Roy F. Lieb spoke about her sensitivity regarding the deformities of her limbs, attributed to the arthritis. He said she wanted to avoid comments by others; therefore, she didn't go out of the house. As a result of her increasing pain, she probably did not leave the house as frequently as before. Also in a 1910 Census, her place of residence was in San Mateo County, thus contributing to the illusion she was a recluse. It is uncertain how long she resided there or why.

It has also been said; she slept in a different room each night to elude and confuse the evil spirits. This is not true; she only slept in two different rooms during her residency. One was at the front of the house, identified as the Daisy bedroom, so-called because of the daisy pattern incorporated into the room's stained glass windows. She slept in this room until the 1906 Earthquake. The other bedroom, occupied after the 1906 Earthquake until her death, overlooked the back garden and the crescent shaped hedge. It was in this room she died.

Other tales told about Mrs. Winchester were just that— tales. The story that she had six safes, one containing her $30,000 gold plated dinnerware is an example. There was only one safe and it was in the Grand Ballroom. When they opened it after her death there was no gold plated dinnerware found. The only things left in the safe were mementos belonging to her husband and daughter.

Perhaps the most widely spread rumor was that Sarah Winchester was mentally unbalanced. Despite rumors to the contrary, she was just the opposite. She was an intelligent, shrewd, articulate, creative, and innovative woman. Had she been crazy, it is doubtful that either her husband or mother-in-law, who died in 1897, would have bequeathed her money or stock in the Winchester Repeating Arms Co. They would have left their money instead to a competent trustee to dole out in monthly installments.

Sarah could not possibly have managed the running of the household with 18-20 domestic servants, 12-18 gardeners and field hands, and 10-22 carpenters had she not been a competent woman. Letters to her lawyer are proof that she was involved with the management of her estate. It took a person in her right mind to oversee numerous employees, the daily construction plans, the gardens, and the workings of the orchards, as well as the sale and distribution of the fruit. She also found time in her busy schedule to give to charities, visit the sick, read, play the organ and piano. Mrs. Winchester spent time researching books for her gardening and drawing plans. A person who was mentally unstable would have never been able to orchestrate all her tasks so effortlessly and efficiently.

A woman who believed she would prolong her own death by continuously building, would never have made a will. Had Sarah been insane, she would never have written such an intricate, carefully planned will. It was said she worked on her will for several years with some difficulty. Sarah wrote her lawyer about her attempt in writing it. "I am in fact, hopelessly bewildered in my inability to make what I desire to do conform to the law." She also wrote that she liked the fact that the money from her relatives trust funds, would come at irregular intervals after that particular relative's death. She mentioned it would keep the hospital administrators from anticipating the money. These words from Mrs. Winchester contradict the belief that she was crazy, in fact; she knew exactly what she was doing. Had she been mentally incompetent she might have spent all her money foolishly, though some believe she was doing just that, lavishing $5.5 million on constructing her house. Yet, she gave money to relatives and charities figuring out exact increments to give to each individual person or charity. With a will so well planned out it is obvious she did things with a definite intent.

Upon researching censuses between 1850 and 1910, it is definite that Sarah Winchester was not insane. On some of the census forms in Connecticut, there was a column to mark if a person was deaf, dumb, blind, or insane. These were never marked in her column. There was no such column in the San Mateo census where she lived in 1910.

It is difficult to discern truth from myth since these stories have been repeated for over a century. No matter what is believed, perhaps we will never know the complete truth about her life, or the real reasons she built the house as she did. What is certain, however; is that Sarah Winchester is one of the most fascinating, mysterious, and most misunderstood women of the 20th Century, if not of all time.

Printed in the United States
46765LVS00007B/427

9 781424 113743